The Incredible Year

THE AUTHOR, *Paris, March, 1945*

The Incredible Year

DONALD J. WILLIS

Iowa State University Press, Ames

This book is dedicated to
my wife, Nona,
and our children, Linda, Bob, and Sandy,
and to the men who served
in the 3rd Armored Division
during World War II

Donald J. Willis was born October 3, 1919, at Pleasantville, Iowa. He was drafted into the United States Army on December 3, 1941, joined the 3rd Armored Division in Camp Polk, Louisiana, and was with it until several months after the end of World War II. He received an Honorable Discharge on October 20, 1945.

The next thirty-seven years of his life were typical of the average American, but during all of this period he thought about writing a book on his experiences with the 3rd Armored "Spearhead" Division during combat in Europe. Upon retiring, he began the account which is in his book. A diary he kept from D-Day on June 6, 1944, to June 6, 1945, provided the outline for his book, which is a true story.

First edition, 1988

Library of Congress Cataloging-in-Publication Data
Willis, Donald J. (Donald James), 1919–
    The incredible year/Donald J. Willis. — 1st ed.
        p.   cm.
    ISBN 0-8138-1036-1
    1. Willis, Donald J. (Donald James), 1919–   . 2. World War. 1939–1945 — Campaigns — Europe. 3. World War, 1939–1945 — Personal narratives, American. 4. United States. Army. Armored Division, Third — History. 5. United States. Army — Biography. 6. Soldiers — United States — Biography. I. Title.
    D756.W49 1988
    940.54'12'73 — dc19

Contents

Preface

IN WRITING THIS BOOK, I have presented one year of my life while serving with the 3rd Armored Division in Europe during World War II. Much of the content has been taken from the diary I kept from June 6, 1944, to June 6, 1945. Also, some of the subjects are from memory.

To set the stage a little, I was single, twenty-two years old, and living in Swan, Iowa, when I was drafted into the army. My training in the 3rd Armored Division was at Camp Polk, Louisiana; the Mojave Desert in California; Camp Pickett, Virginia; and the Indiantown Gap Military Reservation in Pennsylvania. Training for this division was very hard and complete, including road marches, obstacle courses, and instruction in the maintenance of equipment and guns and in such subjects as aircraft recognition, camouflage, and chemical warfare. Everyone had to qualify on guns in our unit. Armor and speed very soon became the key words in the division. After this training, we were convoyed to England, where we were based at Warminster during the big buildup of forces before D-Day.

This is my story as I lived it as a private on the long, hard road from Omaha Beach in Normandy to Dessau in Germany on the Elbe River. There is no glory in war, as you will find in reading my book. The only real heroes are the fallen ones.

The men of the 3rd Armored "Spearhead" Division came to know very soon the horrors of war. But being witness to it, they soon realized that slavery is even more terrible. The long, bloodstained road covering hundreds of miles took its grim toll during their journey. We, the survivors, have not forgotten, and each year a Spearhead reunion is held to honor and pay tribute to our buddies who paid the supreme sacrifice.

Donald J. Willis

Acknowledgments

I would like to acknowledge the assistance of Col. Andrew Barr (Ret.), 3rd Armored Division Headquarters, Washington, D.C., and Lt. Col. Haynes Dugan (Ret.), 3rd Armored Division Headquarters, Shreveport, Louisiana, for their knowledge and cooperation, and of my wife, Nona, for her understanding during the preparation of this book.

Introduction

by Alan M. Schroder

DONALD WILLIS'S WARTIME DIARY offers a glimpse of much of the equipment and many of the tactics employed by the American and German forces on the western front in World War II. He was assigned to the crew of an M3 half-track (usually shortened to "track" in his diary). This was a lightly armored vehicle like a heavy truck with the usual front wheels but with tracks instead of rear wheels. Willis's assignment was to operate the .50-calibre machine gun installed in a ring mount next to the driver. This mounting, which Willis refers to as the "turret," was designed to serve as an antiaircraft weapon against enemy dive-bombers or fighters. The Luftwaffe had made extensive use of close air support in earlier campaigns in the war, but by the time of the Normandy invasions the Allies had gained such complete air superiority that the Luftwaffe was seldom able to attack targets in this way. Instead, Willis employed the half-track's .50-calibre machine gun as an antipersonnel weapon in defending against German counterattacks by infantry or infantry supported by armor and in general suppressive fire against suspected locations of German snipers. He also had a Browning automatic rifle as a personal weapon. The half-track's equipment also included a .30-calibre, tripod-mounted machine gun for use when the antitank gun the half-track towed was emplaced in a defensive position, as in a roadblock.

This antitank gun — a 57 mm gun — was apparently employed in conjunction with a second half-track and towed gun. The gun crew was first assigned to defend a battery of 105 mm self-propelled guns and later the 3rd Armored Division's headquarters company. These assignments reflected American antitank doctrine at this stage of the war, as outlined by Charles Baily in his book *Faint Praise: American Tanks and Tank Destroyers during World War II*. American analysts' conclusions, based on the Allies' earlier experiences in North Africa, were that front-line units would be able to defend themselves against German tanks and assault guns (which were heavily armored, self-propelled guns that resembled turretless tanks) using towed antitank guns firing from concealed positions. The more heavily gunned and mobile tank destroyers, which were similar in appearance to tanks but were lightly armored and had turrets with open tops, were expected to serve as a mobile reserve to stop major counterattacks by German tanks that penetrated, or threatened to penetrate, the front lines.

But experience in the Normandy campaign demonstrated that none of the towed antitank guns in the American arsenal were very effective against the frontal armor of the tanks the Germans were then employing. Towed guns also lacked the mobility to maneuver to allow their gun crews to obtain shots against the lighter armor on the sides of the German tanks, which they could penetrate. As a result, American field commanders began to call for, and receive, permission to disperse their tank destroyers among the front-line units to give them the protection towed guns could not. This proved effective in conditions like that of the hedgerow country of Normandy, where the German army employed only small numbers of tanks in localized counterattacks against the American forces. At that time most of its armor units were committed farther east, in the British sector. This tactic would prove disastrous, however, in later actions like the Ardennes campaign (the Battle of the Bulge), in which the Germans committed massive numbers of tanks against the same defense.

Willis sometimes remarked (as in his entry for June 26, 1944) that he felt more secure when his gun crew was joined by M4 Sherman tanks or the division's M10 tank destroyers, which indicates that he recognized the limitations of his crew's own 57 mm gun. Actually, he should not have felt much more secure, because none of the guns Americans used as antitank weapons was very effective against the frontal armor of the newer German tanks like the Panther and Tiger. As with the towed guns, the Shermans and tank destroyers were effective against these tanks only when they could use their superior mobility to maneuver for a flank shot, and they could not use this mobility if they were sitting around a towed-gun emplacement. Not until early 1945 did the 3rd Armored Division begin to receive a heavy tank that was more a match for the German tanks it was facing. This was the M26 Pershing, whose 90 mm gun could better penetrate the German frontal armor, though the tank itself was underpowered for its weight.

In terms of its own survivability, the Sherman tank's armor was too light to be very effective in protecting it against the 76 mm gun of the Panther tank, let alone the 88 mm gun of the Tiger or the 128 mm gun of the *Jagdtiger*, a very heavy tank destroyer. The Sherman could use its greater speed and more rapidly traversing turret to overcome this disadvantage in the summer and fall of 1944, but when deep mud took much of the Sherman's advantage away in the late fall and winter of 1944–1945, increasing numbers of Shermans were knocked out. Further, the Sherman quickly acquired a reputation for "brewing up," or starting on fire, when its armor was penetrated. Willis notes both situations in his diary entries during these months.

For all its faults, the Sherman was the mainstay of the American armored divisions, and Willis mentions some of the equipment that the Army attached to it for special purposes. In Normandy, for example, the army attached bulldozer blades to the front of many tanks in response to the omnipresent hedgerows, which were mounds of earth and densely entwined roots that forced any tank that tried simply to roll over them to expose its thinly armored underside to enemy antitank fire. The bulldozer blades allowed tanks to smash directly through the hedgerows with no increase in vulnerability. A similar effect was achieved by welding several plow-shaped teeth onto the front hull itself. Other special-purpose equipment Willis describes includes the flail, a series of lengths of chain attached to a rapidly revolving cylinder on a mount attached to the front of the tank, and a series of large rollers on a similar mount and designed for the same purpose: to detonate antipersonnel and antitank mines and thus to provide a clear path for advancing infantry and vehicles.

A very good friend of the American front-line soldier, and one whose help Willis repeatedly acknowledges, was the P-47 Thunderbolt fighter-bomber of the Ninth Tactical Air Command. The Thunderbolt was armed with two 500- or 1,000-pound bombs under the wings and possibly a 500-pound bomb under the fuselage, and these proved very effective against German armor in a close air support role. In place of the bombs, the Thunderbolt could also be armed with racks for ten 5-inch rockets, though Willis never mentions the P-47's use of rockets in his diary. Beyond this, the plane's eight .50-calibre machine guns were deadly against lighter vehicles and infantry. Whether ranging the German front-line areas in search of targets of opportunity or responding directly to requests from radio-equipped forward observers (whom Willis refers to as "ground crews"), the P-47s softened up the German defenses against many Allied advances and blunted the force of many German counterattacks, as Willis often describes. Beyond his vantage point, however, the Thunderbolts also patrolled German rear areas, interdicting the railroad and road transportation of troops and materiel moving to the front.

The Thunderbolts were, of course, affected much more by bad weather than were the ground forces. Low overcast or fog could ground them as far as close air support was concerned, as it did during the crucial early days of the Battle of the Bulge. The importance of this loss to the troops on the ground is revealed by the feeling of apprehension Willis records in his diary whenever bad weather takes the P-47s out of the skies and the sense of relief in his diary entries when clear weather brings them back.

As mentioned earlier, the German forces were almost totally lacking in this type of support by the time of the Normandy invasion. German dive-bombers like the Ju-87 Stuka had earlier proved to be very effective on the eastern front, but they were too slow to survive against the much faster British and American fighters on the western front. Further, the massive Allied strategic bombing raids had drawn the German fighter arm into costly defensive actions that destroyed the German fighters much faster than they could be replaced. On February 16, 1945, Willis mentions sighting a German jet fighter for the first time. This was the Me-262, a twin-engine jet that first saw action in the fall of 1944 and that was much superior to any aircraft the Allies had to oppose it. The Me-262 might have been a serious threat to Allied air superiority if it had been produced in sufficient numbers, but Hitler became so enthusiastic about its performance as a fighter in early demonstrations that he insisted that various capabilities be incorporated into it (including those of a dive-bomber that Willis notes). This delayed production so that only a few hundred aircraft were ever completed, and this limited number of planes did not have a major effect on the war.

For the most part, the Luftwaffe was able to provide only relatively small night bombing raids against the Allied lines. Although such raids could be terrifying — and deadly — to the soldier on the ground, a fact that Willis records, such bombing was neither extensive enough nor accurate enough to do serious damage to the Allied forces because they could rapidly replace their losses from the steady flow of troops, ordnance, and supplies that arrived regularly from supply dumps in the rear. Willis chronicles this flow in his diary, especially after January 25, 1945, when he was permanently transferred to duty on the 3rd Armored Division's resupply convoys.

Both sides, of course, made extensive use of artillery in both an offensive and defensive role, though the Allies again had a preponderance in numbers. Though the Germans had a wide range of artillery, most of the bombardments Willis records would have come mainly from 75 mm infantry guns and 105 mm field guns. The deadly 88 mm antiaircraft gun converted for use with both high-explosive and armor-piercing shells against ground targets was very effective, but it was much less numerous than the reports of American troops would indicate. The troops' fully justified respect for the 88 tended to cause them to mentally convert any concealed towed gun into an 88 and a Panther tank (with its less effective 75 mm gun) into an 88-armed Tiger.

German units were also armed with a variety of mortars, which would have accounted for some of the incoming rounds Willis sought to survive when his antitank gun crew was positioned near the front lines. Mortars, in fact, accounted for a high proportion of all Allied casualties on the western front. Particularly nerve-wracking were the multibarreled mortars called *Nebelwerfers*, whose bombs — which the troops called "screaming meemies" — had high-pitched sirens to add a psychological aspect to their explosive effect.

Willis also occasionally mentions bombardments by German railway guns. These guns, generally ranging from 203 to 280 mm, saw some use on both the eastern and western fronts, and their enormous rounds — called "flying boxcars" by the American troops — could have a devastating effect in a limited area. But they were designed mainly for use in siege operations against heavy fortifications, and they were never produced in great numbers.

Finally, Willis commonly mentions seeing a German "robot bomb" passing overhead on its way west. These were the low-flying V-1 rockets that the Germans used first against English cities and later against European cities under Allied control. The rockets were never accurate enough for use against battlefield targets; so the only direct effect they had on Allied front-line troops came from malfunctioning rockets that fell far short of their targets.

On the American side, the most common artillery pieces were the 105 mm and 155 mm guns, both of which had a towed and a self-propelled version. Willis's antitank gun crew and another gun crew were originally assigned to provide protection for a battery of M7 105 mm self-propelled guns, which were 105 mm guns mounted on a cutdown version of the M4 Sherman tank chassis and supplied with some light armor to protect the crew. Later, the 3rd Armored Division also received a complement of heavier and longer-range 155 mm self-propelled guns and even some 240 mm guns. The latter were so large that they required one specially designed transporter to carry the gun mounting and another to carry the barrel. Each was pulled by a tracked vehicle, either its own tractor or an available tank. The gun was also accompanied by a twenty-ton crane used to assemble and help emplace it.

To locate the targets for this artillery, the division's batteries employed radio-equipped forward observers, who transmitted the map coordinates of the target and any required corrections when the initial rounds were off-target or when a mobile target had moved. In this way they were much like the "ground crews" Willis describes for the P-47 fighter-bomber missions, and his gun crew was sometimes assigned to protect both types of spotters.

In his wartime diary, then, Willis presents the individual soldier's view of combined-arms operations on the western front from shortly after D-Day until the end of the war in Europe in May 1945. As Willis's diary entries indicate, the Allied infantry and armor worked closely together in their advance, and they were supported by division and corps artillery and the fighters and fighter-bombers of the air arm. Similarly, the German army, which by 1944 had become expert in the tactics of mobile defense and local counterattack, used its own infantry, armor, and artillery (and the Luftwaffe's remaining aircraft) to slow the Allied advance. Once the Allies had secured a firm foothold on the Continent in the period immediately after D-Day, the preponderance of their military forces made the ultimate outcome certain, but this did not mean that the twelve months from June 1944 to May 1945 were any less difficult — or deadly — for the soldier like Willis, who found himself at the point of the Allied spearhead.

The Incredible Year

JUNE 5

Leaves this make the year. I am one year older. To me it turned a lifetime.

1944 JUNE 6

This was it at last. The big day we are still in England. Missed the first wave, Lucky.

JUNE 7

Another day finds us getting more equipment and testing. Most kept closed to the radio.

ayed
one
new boat

3

non answered
with today.

UNE 4

getting my
of guard.
to think I
a good
editor.

1
The Beginning

WILLIS BEGINS HIS DIARY on D-Day, June 6, 1944. His gun crew, as part of the 67th Field Artillery Battalion, was encamped near Warminster in Wiltshire, about ninety miles west southwest of London. The 3rd Armored Division, to which his battalion was attached, was not part of the initial Allied invasion force but was instead an element of the massive buildup of troops and equipment scheduled to be landed in the beachhead established by the invasion forces. By mid-June the division was on its way to the Channel port of Southampton, but the passage across was delayed by the worst Channel gale in many years, a gale that not only upset the timetable for the buildup but seriously damaged the artificial harbors the Allies had constructed at the Normandy beachhead and thus caused delays in the landing of troops and materiel until the French port of Cherbourg was captured in late June. Much of the wreckage Willis described as his LST approached the Normandy beaches was, in fact, the result of this gale rather than the destruction caused on D-Day itself.

When Willis's unit landed on June 24 it was moved immediately to the heart of the fighting on the front lines near. St.-Lô. The Germans were very much interested in blunting the expansion of the beachhead and used their artillery to do so. Their reaction gave Willis his first taste of the hours of terrified inactivity in a foxhole, hoping simply to survive the current air or artillery bombardment that was to characterize so much of his life on the western front. Beginning in mid-July, Willis also found himself in the middle of one of the major German counterattacks designed to knife through the Allied lines and split them into isolated sectors that could be destroyed one by one.

Tuesday, June 6, 1944   Invasion! At last the day we all knew was coming has arrived. Everyone is grim as we listen to the news on the radio.

I'm located in England with the 3rd Armored Division. We have been stationed here since the fall of 1943. I've been assigned to the crew of a towed 57 mm antitank gun in the 67th Field Artillery Battalion. There are six men on our crew. Walter Stackowski from Pennsylvania is our gunner. The driver of our half-track, Otto Reicharbt, hails from Texas. The two loaders are Lester Glatt, from New Orleans, and James Habr, who is from my home state — Iowa. The fifth member of our crew is a red-headed Irishman named Dooligan. Everyone calls him "Father," a name he acquired years ago. Father is a legend among the boys here and is well liked by all. We are fortunate to have him as a member of our gun crew. He is a machine gunner on the .30-calibre gun. My job is in the .50-calibre gun turret.

Everyone realizes we have been lucky in missing the first landing on D-Day. However, we also know that it is only a matter of time until our division will be on the way across the English Channel, bound for the beaches of Normandy.

Wednesday, June 7, 1944   It is very foggy, and a fine mist covers the area. Rain seems to be always falling in England. Our battalion finds it is hard to keep our clothing and gear dry while bivouacked out on the downs in pup tents.

The sounds are many. Wave after wave of heavy bombers comes into view, and we hear the muted distant rumbling of bombardment. Looking around at one another, I wonder if we have the same thoughts. How many of us will come back? Everyone is very nervous, but all try to hide our true feelings.

Thursday, June 8, 1944   Crawling out of my pup tent, I find the foul weather is still with us. It is much quieter out in the field than back at the barracks. Some of the troops have been hunting the abundant deer in the nearby woods. Everyone has been warned not to kill any of the king's deer. However, I have been hearing shots from the forests. As evening draws near, I observe several deer carcasses hanging from the trees. No one is taking the ban seriously, as we know nothing will keep us from going to France.

Friday, June 9, 1944   Have no idea when we will be moving from these fields of England. The suspense is terrible! Much worse than I imagined when we talked previously about our reactions when the invasion finally came. We have nothing to do but wait. So many things run through my mind. Home seems to be a million miles away in another world.

Some of my idle time is spent playing poker. I'm lucky, as my money keeps piling up. Doesn't really matter, though, as our division is restricted and cannot go into any of the towns.

Saturday, June 10, 1944   Irish McMahon and I had a long conversation today. He is a good friend from Clare, Iowa. We went on several furloughs together back in the States. We decided to go see each other's parents if one of us never returns. Irish is assigned to an ammunition train, as is another buddy of mine, Bowden, whose home is Alice, Texas. Bowden and I went on most of our passes together while in the States.

Most of us seem to be in good spirits, or else putting on a good act, as I am trying to do. We must make the best of our predicament as we sit and wait.

Sunday, June 11, 1944   Colonel Edward Berry, our battalion commander, informed us that it is only a short time until we will be in France. There is no doubt now but that the worst lies ahead of us. I'm hoping for the best and trying to keep a positive attitude. However, at times it takes all of my courage to look ahead. We have been told there will be plenty to do when we land on the beach in Normandy.

Monday, June 12, 1944   I'm on KP again. They must have figured this would be the last time they would be able to use me for awhile. Since I'm part of the crew on the antitank gun, I'll not be very close to the kitchen truck. Already we have been informed that both guns will be for the protection of the M7 105 mm self-propelled firing batteries. Our antitank guns will be set up ahead of our battalion. Sounds like a suicide alarm system to me.

Tuesday, June 13, 1944   Mail call brought me several letters, and I answered as many as I could. Letter writing may be difficult once we land in France.

The sun has been elusive for several days, and a cold rain prevails. The weather seems to further dampen one's outlook on a rather dismal and gloomy future. Each day I try to reassure myself that all will turn out fine in the long run.

Wednesday, June 14, 1944   General Doyle Hickey, the commander of Combat Command A, gave us our last-minute instructions. He told us that we are ready in both men and equipment. He seemed to be much more confident than I am. I'll never be ready, but there is nothing one can do to change anything.

Several of my buddies act as if they are in a hurry to cross the Channel. I am not looking forward to the trip. I keep thinking of an old saying my Dad had: "Be careful you don't get out of the frying pan into the fire." I have a feeling in my gut that that is right where we are heading.

Thursday, June 15, 1944   At last we receive orders to move out of bivouac, and morning finds our division on the roads leading to the port. Peering out from behind my gun, I see our large convoy stretching for miles along the dusty roads.

The English people wave and shout words of encouragement as they line the streets of the small villages. I am not sure if they are friendly or just glad to be rid of us. I doubt if there is a drink to be found on the whole island. A number of sad English girls are being left behind. I am not overjoyed at leaving England myself, as some good times were had while on pass.

Friday, June 16, 1944   Late in the day, our convoy arrives at the port of Southampton on the southern coast. On leaving our vehicles, I look out over the harbor and at the hundreds of various-sized ships. I'm sure they have one for us.

As night falls, we are marched into a compound with armed guards on duty. Doesn't look as if anyone will be going on a pass tonight. We are treated to an English meal from their rations. After a few days of this food, we will no doubt be glad to move on.

Saturday, June 17, 1944   We are very busy loading onto an LST. Yes, they had no trouble finding a vessel for us to cross the channel. Looking out from this flat-bottom reminds me of how a mouse might feel upon the ocean sitting on a shingle.

I didn't believe we could be so crowded. We have been ordered to stay close to our guns and vehicles. Couldn't move if we wanted to, as there is no extra room. This tub sure isn't a luxury liner, but we are not going on a pleasure cruise.

The navy crew is treating us very well. We have ice cream for the first time since leaving the States. The sailors will not tell us much about the invasion or the beaches. Some informed us that what lies ahead is no picnic. They have made several trips, and very few will even talk of what happened.

Sunday, June 18, 1944   Upon crawling out from beneath our track and gun, I see we are still in the harbor. We hear our trip is being delayed as there are no life jackets on this ship. No one knows what happened to them, but this news doesn't sound good. We learn several of the other vessels are also without safety gear and that it will be some time before the ships can sail.

Monday, June 19, 1944   I awoke this morning to the noise of high winds and torrential rain. The worst storm in years has hit the English Channel. We are concerned about our troops already on the beaches in this horrible storm. Sure are lucky we weren't on our way in this cracker box. Even the weather seems to be against us.

Tuesday, June 20, 1944   We certainly are eating good while with the navy. Don't believe I could have survived another day on English rations. I will never complain about American food again.

Hardly have room to sleep on this tub, but at least we are not out in the weather. They are not wasting any space getting us across the Channel.

Wednesday, June 21, 1944   This morning we had our first boat drill. I really don't understand the reason, as this flat-bottom would sink in about one minute. We received orders to stay by our gun during the boat ride. There is no room to move, anyway. Morale seems to be good, and the pride in our division is outstanding. How we react after we land remains to be seen.

Thursday, June 22, 1944   Early morning finds our convoy moving out to sea. There aren't very many vessels in our fleet. The coast of England fades away as we gain speed. The English Channel is calm after the storm of the past few days. There is a quietness among the troops, each with his own private thoughts.

No time to enjoy the ride, as we are kept busy checking our guns and equipment. This is good, as we must be ready when we land in France. Each man has received D and K rations, plus PX rations, motion sickness capsules, and vomit bags. We are as ready as we will ever be.

There are a large number of planes in the sky over us. Everyone hopes that they are friendly aircraft.

Friday, June 23, 1944   As dawn breaks, I see the beach directly ahead of our convoy. It is unusually quiet, which gives me an eerie feeling. There are more sunken ships than ships afloat in these waters. Many things are in the water that should not be there. Smashed tanks, broken equipment, and metal fragments are laying in the brine of Omaha Beach. Behind us in the moist air of the English Channel is the invasion armada, an unbelievable display of power. Warships of all sizes are offshore, now silent, but mute testimony of the terrible battle which took place here. They are grim reminders of what is yet to come.

Barrage balloons sway in the air as P-47 Thunderbolt fighter-bombers zoom from a newly built airstrip close to the beach.

Saturday, June 24, 1944   Gazing out from the LST, I know our voyage has ended. The activity almost staggers me as I realize the enormous size of the Allied invasion. Thousands of engineers are working on the floating piers offshore. I notice a steady stream of German troops, captured in the early fighting, marching down to the beach to board the outgoing ships. It is near dusk when we are finally unloaded and join the long line of American infantry trudging wearily ashore up the muddy road which leads inland. We are fortunate to be riding. Later, we stop to remove waterproofing from our vehicles. There is no doubt now but that we are in France to stay. We move slowly until midnight and spend the rest of the night trying to sleep.

Sunday, June 25, 1944   Normandy! How can I describe where we have landed? A flat, junglelike terrain before St.-Lô. The lush foliage of early summer makes visibility near zero, and the high, earthbound hedgerows partition each small field. Due to the terrain, German defense is made simple and Allied attack is becoming a nightmare.

Our commands are finding that the Krauts have very wisely zeroed all crossroads of American activity. They have plenty of field guns, which they use ceaselessly, and their ammunition supply seems inexhaustible.

It is here and now we get our first taste of battle. The

front line is only six miles from the beach, and the machine-gun fire we hear is not practice. Very soon we learn there is no glory in war. Death strikes friend and foe alike. For the first time, we hear the spine-chilling shriek of incoming mail and the bell crash of a close hit, followed by the horrifying screams of our stricken men before the dust and debris finally settle. We see death in its most violent form as man is pitted against man to survive by the destruction of his enemy. It is in these hedgerows that we smell the terrifying scent of battle. The fresh, green smell of crushed shrubbery and the pungent odor of flame nearly choke us.

The battle for a little French village named Villiers Fossard is our first baptism of fire, but it is only the beginning. Here we count our first dead.

Monday, June 26, 1944   Our chief gunner tells us that we have been ordered to move closer to the front line. Arriving at our destination, we very quickly dig in our antitank gun for defense. We can see the Germans very plainly through the trees a short distance away. As I gaze close up at my enemy, my feelings are a mixture of fear and curiosity.

It is very quiet and all are trying to keep it that way. There are several Sherman tanks from the 33rd Armored Regiment with us. Everyone feels more secure by their presence, as they carry larger guns and have more armor.

The only member of our crew who isn't scared is Father, who just takes another drink of cognac.

Tuesday, June 27, 1944   After finally getting to sleep last night, I was awakened very quickly by the roar of many planes. Enemy dive-bombers attacked our beachhead for several hours. At first, all were very scared, as we thought they were dropping paratroopers. We observed many fires and learned that the troops at the beach suffered heavy losses in troops and equipment.

With the coming of dawn, we see many dead livestock

in our area, killed by the weapons of war. The smell is terrible, but we have no time to bury them. We are too busy providing shelter for ourselves. The few French that are seen are not very friendly or are very frightened — as I am.

Wednesday, June 28, 1944   Near morning it started to rain again and I found myself in a bed of water. After getting soaked, I gave up trying to get any sleep the rest of the night. I kept thinking of my dry bed back home. Sure hope we get to some high ground soon.

We pay a very high price for every foot of ground we fight for and occupy. We learn quickly that our life in France is rough and extremely dangerous. No one gives us anything. It is a very high price we are paying as we very slowly move ahead.

Thursday, June 29, 1944   Morning finds our field artillery batteries firing in support of the 29th Infantry Division. Barrage after barrage of shells from our large guns hits the enemy lines. After several hours, some of our tanks creep forward.

We now begin to understand how the Germans have been able to conquer nearly all of Europe. There is no doubt in anyone's mind; this war will not be over soon. We find every hedgerow opening zeroed in by antitank and machine-gun fire. It is suicide to attempt a frontal assault, as the Krauts are too well dug in by their fortifications.

Our maintenance battalion attached dozers to some of our tanks, which are helping to crash through the hedgerows around the small fields.

Friday, June 30, 1944   Morning finds our forces continuing the attack in support of the infantry. Every hedgerow taken is only by the guts and blood of the doughs [doughboys]. We see firsthand the terrible results of war as our buddies are struck down by the enemy.

In the hedgerows, life is very rough on all of us, but the living conditions of the doughboys are by far the worst of the lot, as their foxholes are full of water most of the time. They often find no place to eat their cold K rations. Added to these dreadful conditions, their casualties are the highest among all the troops.

I never knew one could get so tired and still not be able to sleep, but it is happening to all of us.

Saturday, July 1, 1944   It will be a long time before I forget this day. We received our first heavy artillery shelling by the enemy forces. Seemed to me it would never end as barrage after barrage of shells fell upon our lines. Many of our tanks and other vehicles were hit and set on fire. Everywhere an inferno of flame could be seen as a heavy pall of black smoke settled around us.

Through the heroic efforts of our medics, many lives are saved. For the first time, we have all come to realize they are extra special. Many Red Cross vehicles are seen on the roads continuously taking care of the wounded. Some of them also become casualties while going into the flame of battle.

By dark, most of the shelling has ceased, but we are so nervous no one can sleep. We stay up most of the night talking, trying to keep our courage up.

Sunday, July 2, 1944   Our crew observed the first dogfight between our planes and the enemy this morning. Each side lost one plane in the encounter. We noticed the tall grass moving rapidly around us, although no wind was blowing, and realized the movement was the result of machine-gun bullets from the planes above us. Quickly we sought shelter under our tracks [half-tracks] and tanks.

Every time we get a break and all seems calm for awhile, the siren wail of the German 88 comes, and it is time to duck again. It's surprising how fast I can dig a hole and crawl in.

Received a letter from my folks at mail call. Have no time to write now, but will try to answer later.

Monday, July 3, 1944   Seems to be quiet around here today. One could almost forget where we are, but not quite. I am going to keep alert just in case something does happen. I'm on a roadblock with my crew and as usual we are alone. Some of us are supposed to be sleeping, but who can rest? We stay awake most of the time.

Several small villages are nearby. However, we have not seen many French since landing at Omaha Beach. Most moved away from the action when the invasion came.

After all of our training in using pup tents, no one uses them over here. It is too much trouble, and we have no time to bother with them. Many times we must move at a moment's notice. At night, without lights, this is quite a feat. We must be able to respond quickly. My submachine gun and gas mask are with me at all times. My iron helmet is as close to my head as my hair.

Tuesday, July 4, 1944   Last night our crew joined a convoy and drove most of the night back to a rest area. Didn't move very far, as most of the time was spent on the road waiting. Our bivouac area is still in range of the heavy guns of the Germans.

Jerry planes were out most of the night while we were on the road. They dropped bombs and flares over a large area. No damage was received by our convoy. Glatt informed us that the enemy was just keeping in practice.

The Fourth of July in France turned out to be much noisier than any I ever experienced back in Iowa.

Wednesday, July 5, 1944   It is fairly quiet now, for a change. I'm taking advantage of the lull by writing some letters home. Also wrote one for a friend, Dan, who can't read or write. He has so many girlfriends it keeps several of us busy answering all of his mail.

The field where we are bivouacked is full of bomb holes. This will save us some time, as we will not have to dig shelters.

Our gun crew has been issued ten-in-one rations,

which we will have to cook while away from the kitchen truck. No one is too pleased with this news. We can survive on cognac if we run out of rations, as Father has laid in an ample supply for our crew. Every time we stop, he is out trading our food for liquor. He seems to be able to smell the beverage no matter where it is located.

Thursday, July 6, 1944   Arrived back at the front as dawn broke. Had very little success trying to sleep on the trip. Machine-gun fire and small-arms exchange announce our arrival at the front line.

Today we received orders that Combat Commands A and B are to launch an attack to the south. Since our crew is part of this force, we will be moving soon. Our crew spent the rest of the day checking all guns and ammunition belts.

Friday, July 7, 1944   The 3rd Armored Division attacked at dawn today. A heavy barrage by our 67th, 54th, and 391st Artillery Battalions preceded the assault. Our 23rd Engineers had to build a bridge at Airel. The enemy managed to destroy the structure three times before our forces could use it for crossing. The German shelling resulted in heavy losses among the engineers.

The 36th Armored Infantry Regiment with tanks from the 32nd and 33rd Armored Regiments are attacking from the bridgehead. We are moving ahead very slowly against heavy enemy resistance.

Our crew is on a roadblock and have dug our gun in for an expected counterattack. We cannot expect any help from our fighter-bombers, as the weather is rainy and overcast. Rumor is we are facing some of Germany's crack panzer divisions. As slowly as we are advancing, I'm sure this information is true.

After examining some of the destroyed enemy tanks, we find their armor is much heavier than the armor on our Shermans. Also, their shells are longer, with more powder. The Germans have very good weapons of war.

Saturday, July 8, 1944   For the first time we are seeing more German prisoners. Our forces have captured quite a number the past few days. Most are ragged and dirty, some are very young. The SS troops are arrogant and fanatical in their loyalty to Hitler. One captured trooper would not accept blood from our medics. After they attempted to help him several times, the young SS soldier died.

It is still very rainy and miserable, which makes the nights very bad, as it is difficult to find a dry place to sleep. Even when we do, it is almost impossible to rest, as the muzzle flashes of the large guns, added to the lightning, turn night into day.

Sunday, July 9, 1944   We are in another field now, which is covered with dead livestock. Dan managed to find a live cow, which he has been milking. This morning he had to make a trip to the beachhead with the ammunition train. While he was away, some of his buddies cut off his milk supply by butchering his cow. Upon his return he was very surprised to find everyone enjoying steak. The cow was still tied to his track, as only the hindquarters were used for food. The evening meal of tender beef was very delightful. However, Dan did not seem too pleased with the turn of events.

Monday, July 10, 1944   One of our half-tracks caught fire this morning and was salvaged before it reached the ammunition. Some of the boys received burns. We try to avoid large fires, as the black smoke gives the enemy a target to zero in on.

Received our first rocket attack from the Germans this morning. The rockets are very deadly and give very little warning before striking.

As evening comes to the hedgerows, there are several P-38s above our positions. This is a very pretty plane. However, the P-47 Thunderbolts are a much greater help to our forces. The Air Corps has its own ground crew here with us to direct their planes when their help is needed.

Tuesday, July 11, 1944   Our forces are still being shelled heavily every day. I am still very nervous and try to overcome it. Normandy is one place where one must keep a clear head at all times. A couple of troopers have been sent back to England, as they could not take the strain here. We are finding it to be no place for the fainthearted.

We found a small pond near the place we have our guns set up. Was thinking of going swimming, but about that time several large shells landed in the center of the little lake. Due to the shelling, we decided to cancel our dip in the water.

Wednesday, July 12, 1944   This morning we found a dead German soldier in the heavy brush. A letter was laying beside him. In it he had written his wife that he was tired of fighting and wanted to go home.

The water in France is terrible tasting, and it must be treated before we can use it. About all we use it for is to make coffee or washing. Nearly everyone drinks cognac when thirsty — which is often. Habr is the only member of our gun crew who does not drink. He seems to be depressed most of the time. Father and I take turns drinking his share of the beverages.

Thursday, July 13, 1944   Received orders and had to move quickly this morning. We have to be ready to move at a moment's notice and wait on no one — be there or be left behind.

A battery of 155 mm self-propelled field artillery is attached to our division. Their guns are much larger than the ones we use. A vast amount of new equipment is coming up from the beach.

Friday, July 14, 1944   The front was quiet for a change, so I managed to write a letter to my folks. Expect something will happen to alter this, as it usually does.

Father tells us that we all worry too much, and I'm sure he is right, but it is hard not to be concerned.

We are with the 9th Infantry Division. They landed on Omaha Beach on D-Day. Some of their troops are now moving up to the front past our roadblock to advance positions on the front line. As I observe this maneuver, one dough in particular catches my attention. In place of a helmet, he is wearing a top hat. Added to his comical appearance, both arms are covered with wristwatches.

Saturday, July 15, 1944   Our crew is awakened before dawn and ordered to move out to an advance roadblock with our antitank gun. Arriving at our destination, we are glad to find another gun crew already there with their large 90 mm gun.

Digging in, we learn the Germans are counterattacking all along the front. We receive very heavy shellfire from the enemy. Our forces are in a very perilous position, as the Krauts are trying to cut off our supply line to the beach. We have no idea where the rest of our battery is, so will have to eat K rations — if we can find the time.

Sunday, July 16, 1944   The weather has cleared enough that our P-47 Thunderbolts are able to help us. Enemy tanks have broken through our lines in one sector. We see where our dive-bombers are strafing very close to our roadblock. All were concerned that our planes were strafing too close until we saw two German tanks in the next hedgerow. The enemy tanks were nearly to us when our bombers scored hits and set them on fire. We feel the heat from the roaring flames of the burning tanks. That is getting a little too close for comfort.

I had heard of hell, but never thought I would see it. However, it must be close by. Fire and flame are everywhere as the heavy black smoke drifts over us.

Our medics in their Red Cross vehicles are busy on the roads bringing out the wounded. There is no slackening as the battle rages into the night hours. The muzzle flashes of the large guns, followed by explosions of shells, are everywhere. Tracers from machine guns arc and flash across the sky and terrain. There is no sleep for anyone this black night as we nervously peer into the smoky mist beside our guns. This is one night not soon to be forgotten.

Monday, July 17, 1944   The situation is critical. Our artillery guns are deafening as salvo after salvo of explosives falls upon the enemy forces. The battle has now become a raging inferno. The black smoke is so dense in places that we can hardly see.

Our ammunition trains are busy trying to keep our batteries supplied. We learn that our orders are to hold our positions. There is no place to go anyway, as the English Channel is but a few miles behind us. We must stop this German attack. There is no other way out for us. No time to eat in this hell hole.

Tuesday, July 18, 1944   Good news! The German counterattack is smashed at last. It was very frightening as we desperately held our ground. The weather cleared some and our planes were able to assist our forces. Many of the heavy tanks of the Germans were left burning after being hit by bombs. The battle lasted three days, but it seemed like three weeks. Everyone looks exhausted after no rest during the attack.

This action we just came through didn't seem to bother Father. He just drank more cognac and calmed the rest of us. This big, red-headed Irishman is like a rock in a sea of shifting sand.

Wednesday, July 19, 1944   Today finds me busy enlarging my bedroom. The Germans cut holes under the hedgerows for safety and sleeping. Then we came and they were forced to leave. In my spare time, I'm making my sleeping quarters more comfortable. The main advantage is that I can keep dry when it rains. Have no idea how much longer we will be here, but I'm going to enjoy the comforts while I can.

Small animals and birds are noticcably absent from the area. The noise has either killed them or frightened them away.

Thursday, July 20, 1944   As today is fairly quiet, I took advantage of the lull and looked up Irish. He is still a member of the crew hauling ammunition from the beach-head. He told me that they were real busy during the battle. I offered to trade places with him, but he didn't think much of the idea. So I'll have to remain here with my crew on our antitank gun. Habr and Glatt would like to get on a gas or ammunition track but have not been able to find anyone eager to trade places with them.

Friday, July 21, 1944   We have been alerted to watch for enemy snipers. The Germans have left suicide squads concealed in the heavy foliage behind our lines. A large number of our troops have been slain by these marksmen. Officers in particular have become their targets. Our command has found a counter-solution in dealing with this dangerous problem. Our 486th Anti-Aircraft Battalion has been ordered to use its rapid-fire machine guns to spray all fields and hedgerows before our troops enter them. This operation has proven to be very effective in reducing this danger, as several snipers have been observed falling from the foliage of the tall trees.

Saturday, July 22, 1944   We are back eating at the kitchen truck again. Our ten-in-one rations are good when we can build a fire to cook. In preparing our meals, we use a gallon can with holes punched in the top half. The fuel is gas mixed with dirt, which makes an extremely hot fire. Our plentiful cooking utensils were liberated along the route.

The Jerries were out last night and bombed the front a few miles from here. Managed to keep me awake for a few hours. We learned today that they just missed a prisoner-of-war camp. Too bad they didn't hit it; it would have saved us a lot of trouble.

We are very close to forward positions as our division regroups. In spite of heavy enemy shellfire, new equipment and supplies continue to pour in from the floating docks at Isigny.

Rumors are that the big show is near, but we have no idea what it is or when the event will take place.

Sunday, July 23, 1944   Last night I saw my first German robot on its trip to England. It's a weird sight to behold, with fire shooting from the tail. I'm sure lucky to be in France.

We had a poison-gas scare this morning. A mad scramble was made for the gas masks. I was fortunate to have mine with me. Some of our troops almost went nuts until they found their masks. Everyone was thankful that it turned out to be a false alarm. We are wearing our gas masks at this time.

Monday, July 24, 1944   Every day brings more of our fighter-bombers patrolling the sky here. We are, however, constantly subjected to strafing and bombing attacks at night. Although there is heavy antiaircraft fire from our guns, we seldom see any enemy planes shot down.

The German bombing attacks, along with the heavy artillery fire, make sleep almost impossible at night. Some of us try to get some rest during the day. The only member of our crew it doesn't affect is our gunner, Stack. He never lets anything interfere with his rest.

Tuesday, July 25, 1944   One of the soldiers on an antiaircraft gun was accidentally shot in the hand. Will be lucky if he doesn't lose it, as the bullet was from a .50-calibre machine gun. He will probably be going home. Stack informed us that maybe this trooper was lucky — after all, he is alive. The answer to his statement lies in the future for the rest of us.

2

The Breakout

WITH THE MAJOR GERMAN EFFORT to eliminate the Normandy beachhead crushed and with a massive concentration of troops and equipment on hand by late July, the next Allied move was a breakout that would convert the beachhead into a rapidly expanding area of liberated France and destroy the defending German forces in the process. The 3rd Armored Division's position west of St.-Lô and its role in the subsequent breakout along the St.-Lô—Coutance road placed Willis in a perfect position to record this action.

The operation, code-named COBRA, began on July 25 with a July 26 saturation bombing of the German defenses west of St.-Lô by 1,800 bombers of the U.S. Eighth Air Force, a spectacle that Willis recorded with awe. In the initial advance, the American armor and infantry met fierce but scattered German resistance and moved steadily forward. Willis himself was appreciative of the role the P-47 fighter-bombers were playing in the pinpoint destruction of German armor that his gun crew would have had to face in the event of a determined counterattack against the COBRA forces. The Germans did, in fact, launch such an attack on August 6, a strike westward to reach the coast of the Bay of Biscay at Avranches and cut off supplies to the American forces of the U.S. First Army south and southeast of this line. The task force that included Willis's gun crew was cut off for a time in this very fluid action, and he was relieved when the encirclement was broken by the tanks and troops of another American task force on the following day.

An interesting sidelight of Willis's diary entries is the changing reaction of the civilians the American forces met in their drive into France. Shortly after his arrival in Normandy, Willis noted that the French civilians were sullen, but by the time of the breakout in late July and August he found the cheering crowds so often seen in newsreels. Willis would see civilian reaction change again when the American forces moved into Germany.

Wednesday, July 26, 1944   Crawling out from under our track, I am greeted by a clear day. We wonder if this

23

could be what we were waiting for, but the suspense does
not last long. From the north comes a swarm of Mustang
fighters. I hear a roar and see wave after wave of our
gigantic heavy bombers, followed by scores of medium
bombers.

Watching this vast spectacle unfold, I see many of the
first wave of bombers are hit and fall out of the sky in
countless numbers of broken pieces. Others explode in the
air, seeming much like rockets back home on the Fourth of
July. The German antiaircraft fire is very heavy at first.
There is no slackening of this air fleet as on they come like
a dreadful pall. On the ground, all have mixed emotions.
Everyone is cheering, although they cannot hear us, but
we are sickened when one of our planes falls. We are several
miles from where the bombs fall; still, the ground is
shaking from the concussion of exploding heavy bombs.

No one doubts now — this is indeed the beginning of
the long-awaited big push. The front is moving up even as
the last air fleets are returning to England. Ahead, advancing over the churned and smoking earth, are the 4th, 9th
and 30th Infantry Divisions. This force is driving into a
disorganized enemy line along the St.-Lô road.

Thursday, July 27, 1944   Dawn finds our columns
driving forward, flanked by the 2nd Armored Division on
the left and the 1st Infantry on our right side. Both are
veteran outfits, having landed on D-Day, besides seeing
action in Africa and Sicily.

Passing through the bombed area, we find total destruction. It is almost unbelievable the devastation of this
area. Smoking ruins mark where villages once stood.
Black smoke still rises from burned-out enemy tanks and
other weapons. Many dead German troops are visible
along the roads and in the fields. This scene has a very
sobering effect on us as our armored columns move ahead
along the dusty roads.

Very soon we again find death in our ranks. The
enemy has very wisely pulled back much of his equipment

and troops. Once more, digging in for another battle, the enemy retreat has stopped. Soon we again hear the all-too-familiar sound of screaming shells as they whistle through the air and explode with deadly accuracy. We all realize the breakthrough was only a softening of the German defenses. By no means is the war going to be over soon.

Friday, July 28, 1944   We are still driving forward against stiffening resistance in favorable weather, which is a large factor in our favor. Our swift advance, with the aid of P-47 Thunderbolt dive-bombers, has caught some of the enemy forces by surprise. Clouds of dust cover the roads until we almost choke; still our attack continues without pause. The fine white dust covers everyone and everything. This, added to the goggles we are wearing, makes us look like aliens from another planet.

Everyone seems to be adjusting much better to this situation. At least I am not as nervous, and some things don't bother me as they did when we first arrived in France. Perhaps I am just numb — the feeling is hard to explain.

The dead enemy along the way rarely rate a passing glance from us. They are just that many Germans we don't have to contend with. But when our buddies are slain, our feelings are much different. All know we have lost a friend.

One's values change when faced with the rigors of combat. The everyday living and sharing of hardships and danger with buddies result in a closeness and trust that would be difficult to duplicate anywhere else.

My main concern is for this war to end and to be around when it does. From the action I have been involved in already, this is not going to be an easy task.

Saturday, July 29, 1944   After traveling a short distance this morning, we pulled into a small field to allow our tanks to pull ahead of us. While waiting, we found a dead American soldier in the heavy bushes. We notified our chaplain, who took him back to the rear area in his peep.

As our spearhead columns drive forward, we see many French civilians. They are now lining our route for miles, throwing flowers. Cool drinks are given to soothe our parched throats. Cognac seems to be their main beverage, which goes down very smoothly. People are laughing and crying at the same time. Many climb on our tanks and other vehicles to ride through the villages with us. The children are very happy as we pass out chocolate bars among them. All the French say they are very glad to see us.

The 2nd Armored Division has cut the enemy escape route. Our fighter-bombers are having a field day. Large convoys of the German forces traveling on the narrow Normandy roads are trapped. All along the battlefront, a pall of smoke marks the Nazi retreat and destruction.

We really appreciate the deadly P-47 Thunderbolts. Working closely with their ground crews, they are saving countless American lives. These planes seem to always travel in groups of four.

Sunday, July 30, 1944   Jerry planes were out last night dropping their bombs. Caught us on the road with no shelter. Surprising how close I can get to Mother Earth. None of our troops were hit, but some of the task forces suffered losses.

Much of the fighting is different, as we are driving into a fluid line. At times all is quiet, and then as we begin to relax all hell breaks loose. That is not to imply we are on a picnic, but this is different from before the breakthrough at St. Lô.

Monday, July 31, 1944   After crossing the Sienne River, we move so rapidly that at times our task force captures some German troops napping and drinking wine in the orchards.

Toward evening, one of our advance units liberates a winery in one of the villages. Each crew receives a case of champagne to quench our thirst, and it is very refreshing.

One town, captured by one task force, is soon reoc-

cupied by German troops. The 703rd Tank Destroyer
Battalion moves up close and with their heavy guns
reduces this stronghold to rubble.

Tuesday, August 1, 1944   Looks as if our Roman
Holiday is over. Resistance is stiffening along the front.
Received a grim reminder this morning after being caught
on a hill in the open by German artillery fire. The enemy
laid down a devastating barrage of shells. This resulted in
heavy losses. This evening our task force moved ahead.

We were told a few days ago that a rest period was near.
Otto tells us that if this is a rest he wants to continue to
fight. Morale is good, as we are now moving much faster.

We captured quite a number of enemy troops the last
few days. Would be great if they would all surrender.

Wednesday, August 2, 1944   Checking our supply of
rations, I find we are rather low, but as for beverages there
is plenty, as Father has traded off nearly all of our food.
However, he did get some homemade bread from a pretty
French lady. So, after borrowing several dozen eggs, we are
now in fine shape. Our meal is delicious after our normal
diet of K rations.

Thursday, August 3, 1944   The French civilians seem
to be very happy as we travel through their villages. We are
handed drinks of liquor that I have never heard of or tasted
before. They seem to have an inexhaustible supply of
spirits, which they insist we taste. Everyone is trying very
hard to lower their supply.

The Nazi sympathizers are paying for their past
friendly relationships with the enemy. We see many women
being shaved of their hair, and this is a very mild treatment. The collaborators caught by the maquis, or Free
French, usually get a one-way trip down the road. The
hatred of these French people for Germans is almost
unbelievable. When we learn of the cruel and inhuman
suffering they have endured the past years, we begin to

understand. Dead soldiers, in particular, seem to arouse their hostility. Upon seeing these slain Germans in the streets, most French will express their feelings by spitting on the dead.

The maquis like to guard the captured enemy, but we must keep our eyes on them or there will be no Germans left alive. We find the Free French to be very good allies.

Friday, August 4, 1944   Last night was a period we will remember for a long time. After a fierce battle in a small village which lasted several hours, our task force moved slowly forward. We encountered so many dead in the streets that we were forced to remove bodies from our path. Fires were raging out of control on both sides of the narrow avenues. Sparks were also dropping on us from the burning buildings. Added to this blazing inferno, German bombers arrived on the scene. We were subjected to aerial attack during the following hours. The night was very long, and most of our beverages were consumed by daybreak.

Saturday, August 5, 1944   I have been trying to catch up on some sleep this quiet morning. Very little rest has been obtained the past few days. But Father and Glatt spend their time checking the natives out for more cognac, since our supply was nearly exhausted.

The sky is being patrolled by a large number of dive-bombers. They do give a feeling of some protection.

Sunday, August 6, 1944   The sky is ablaze with the flash of many guns, as the enemy is counterattacking along a large area of the front.

The bridge over the Varenne River is seized by the 1st Infantry troops. Soon they have established a bridgehead on the far side. Our troops cross the river, where we spend some time talking to the people. We are treated to a new drink, which is called calvados. It is reputed to be made of ground-up hand grenades. After sampling this wine, I will have to agree that this information is definitely true.

Finally some good news — we are all to have some rest, take a bath, and wash our clothes in a small creek nearby. Unfortunately, that news is turning out to be false. There will be no time for baths, rest, or anything else. We are ordered to climb back into our fighting machines.

Monday, August 7, 1944   Today we are told that the enemy has launched a full-scale attack to reach the sea at Avranches. The Germans, using heavy tanks and a concentration of artillery fire, have penetrated the line of one of our infantry divisions.

Received orders to move out, and quickly our task force was on the road. While moving into position, we are shelled by enemy artillery fire which threatens to cut off our supply line. The Germans must be using larger guns, as the shells sound like trains passing over us. To give some added excitement, the Jerries bombed and strafed our forces at noon.

Tuesday, August 8, 1944   We are told to move our antitank gun closer to the front to help protect the forward observer. We are very close to the action and have plenty of excitement without looking for it. After getting a closer look at the German tanks, I certainly don't like what I see. The nearer they are the bigger they seem.

Although we are being shelled heavily and suffer repeated bombing raids at night, our forces are holding firm. However, we suffer heavy losses.

Wednesday, August 9, 1944   At dawn we receive some very grim news. Our small force is surrounded. I certainly don't like the looks of this situation.

Orders came over the radio to dig in and hold on until we get help. The enemy has recaptured a town behind us. Our gun crew is barricaded with some Sherman tank crews and troops of infantry. Our forward observers are still directing fire from our heavy guns upon the attacking enemy. Peering out from behind my gun turret, I can see our Thunderbolts dive-bombing and strafing the German lines nearby.

Everyone is alert as darkness descends upon us. There will be no sleep among our small force tonight. It is very nervewracking to know the Germans are on all sides.

Thursday, August 10, 1944   As morning comes, our small group is happy to see Sherman tanks from another task force rolling into our area. Losses were heavy while we were holding our positions against overwhelming enemy forces.

We are back eating at the kitchen truck again. Otto managed to talk one of our cooks out of some fresh bread. If we are isolated again, we will have some bread and wine, at least.

Gazing to the west of our position, I view the setting sun, which is red as blood before it disappears over the horizon. Could this be an omen of what lies ahead for us?

Friday, August 11, 1944   Good news! Orders are for our division to pull back a few miles for some rest and to regroup. Everyone needs sleep, as all are exhausted. If I can relax, I'm going to take advantage of this lull.

It has been a tough grind since the breakthrough at St.-Lô. However, the past two months have had a sobering effect on us. Perhaps we are getting used to the grind of war. I am sure something else has happened to us. Our troops are more quiet and certainly more disciplined than when we came ashore at Omaha Beach. Death is no stranger now, as we see it every day in every conceivable manner. It has been very bitter and costly training. We who have survived are now a crack team.

We are informed that the new commander of the 3rd Armored Division is General Maurice Rose. He assumed command on August 7.

3
The Argentan–Falaise Gap

AFTER A BRIEF REST, the 3rd Armored Division was ordered to move about twenty-five miles southeast to the Mayenne area in preparation for a northeastward push to encircle units of the German Seventh Army, Fifth Panzer Army, and Panzer Group Eberbach in a pocket. Logically speaking, the German forces should no longer have been in the pocket. The success of the American breakout and push south and east demonstrated to the German field commanders that a controlled withdrawal was the only reasonable alternative to the loss of a major part of the German forces in the west. Hitler, however, would allow no such retreat. Finally, on August 16 Field Marshal Günther von Kluge, the German commander in chief in the west, personally ordered the retreat to begin. By then, however, it could be nothing more than an uncoordinated, headlong dash to the Seine.

The Allied failure to close the Argentan–Falaise, however, has often been considered equally inexplicable. The combination of a very slow advance southward from Caen to Falaise by the Canadian First Army and the American adherence to an agreed boundary line between the American and British forces near the town of Argentan left a gap of some ten miles through which thousands of German troops poured — though they were forced to abandon much of their equipment and most of their vehicles in the pocket. Military historians have traditionally concluded that the Allied failure to close the gap was a major blunder, but recently some have concluded that a narrow line of Allied forces could not have held the pocket closed against a determined escape effort by the tens of thousands of German troops. Between the two views, Willis's experiences would certainly support the latter.

After the destruction of the Falaise pocket in mid-August, however, the American forces moved very rapidly eastward again. Between August 21 and September 2, as Willis records, General Omar Bradley's 12th Army Group sped across northern France and into Belgium, capturing Mons, south of Brussels, in early

September. After the debacle at Falaise, German resistance was very weak and disorganized; the German forces could not, in fact, retreat fast enough to stay ahead of the advancing American mechanized columns.

Saturday, August 12, 1944   Rest periods are never very long, as we have orders that a new drive is near. At our briefing, we learn that a large army of the enemy are trying to escape back into Germany. The 3rd Armored Division will drive north to meet the British in an effort to cut off the Germans' route of retreat.

Since the weather is clear, all hope we will receive assistance from our fighter-bombers. With this hazardous mission ahead, we definitely need all the help we can get.

Sunday, August 13, 1944   Our march orders come and after a hurried, cold, K ration breakfast, we climb into our war wagons. By sunrise our convoy is on the dusty roads heading north. Our gun crew is with one of the spearheads leading the attack.

Very little resistance is met as we drive forward. Again crowds of French stand in the bright sunshine along our route of advance. Flowers and large bottles of cognac are thrust into our eager grasp. The drinks are very refreshing after our long, dusty ride. Very little war has come this way, as nothing is disturbed.

Near evening our forces stop for the night and bivouac. We find that our journey this hot, dry day in August has been over fifty miles.

Monday, August 14, 1944   I am awakened very suddenly to the sound of exploding shells and machine-gun fire. Soon we discover the front is all around us. A terrific tank battle is raging closeby. Flames can be seen marking the site of numerous hits, and they are followed by heavy black smoke, which darkens the sky as it rolls over the battlefield. Our firing batteries are forced to shoot directly at the oncoming German armor. The enemy forces are very close. The stench of death is in the air.

We are ordered to move out to another roadblock back of an inn. Upon arriving, we very quickly dig in our gun while Father sets up his machine gun behind a high bank. We are joined by some Sherman tanks. We find that our group is separated from the rest of our unit. There are no French to be seen, as they have wisely moved away from the action.

Father noticed a large cellar under the inn and, investigating, he found a large door, which he broke open. Inside, he was overjoyed to discover, were barrels of cognac. Needless to say, all jugs and canteens were filled. We may have to dump some rations in order to provide room for all this wine. Our friends on the tanks are also thirsty, so we will be able to use all of the liquor.

As the long day drags on, we discover our task force is surrounded by German armor. Our P-47 Thunderbolt dive-bombers seem like angry bees diving in their strafing and bombing attacks upon the enemy lines. But soon we find our forces are in a very perilous situation. The heavy enemy tanks are reinforced by SS infantry, who don't believe in surrendering and usually fight to the death.

Although our forces had some rough action in the hedgerows, we are now faced with a worse development. Our wounded cannot be evacuated, as transportation is impossible. Red Cross vehicles are everywhere on the field of battle; their heroic efforts save many lives. All we have time for are the immediate problems.

Tuesday, August 15, 1944   The stars and moon were absent as I took my turn at guard early in the morning hours. Crouched low behind my machine gun, I was startled to hear a noise very faintly in front of my barricade. I had decided to waken one of my crew when Father crawled up behind my position at the gun. Together we waited until the noise was very close. In the darkness we could barely make out the silhouette of two forms crawling toward us. Knowing there was no time to inform our crew, we both acted accordingly. Soon the chatter of machine-gun fire broke the silence of the night air as we sought to stop the sneak attack of the enemy. The rest of our crew, along with our friends in their tanks, joined in with their weapons.

Everyone stayed awake the rest of the night, but we had no more trouble. As the gray dawn showed in the east, we discovered several dead Germans close to our defenses.

Later, we found that an SS patrol had worked its way into the positions of our tank destroyer battalion last night. They were able to capture one officer and several enlisted men. They were found dead later, except for one soldier who managed to escape. I sure am glad I stayed awake last night.

The French who own the inn returned today and were very upset after finding their barrels of cognac were empty. Father took up a collection among all of our troops. After receiving a helmet full of bills, they were very happy. The innkeepers didn't want to take all of the money, but Father brushed their protests aside and made them take all of it, as money means nothing to us.

Wednesday, August 16, 1944   Our forces are still encountering heavy opposition from a very stubborn enemy. We have been able to advance some, but very slowly. Our 703rd Tank Destroyer Battalion, although greatly outnumbered by the foe, managed to destroy several heavy German tanks and hold a key road and rail junction.

As night comes, we are forced to move our convoy through a burning village. We pick our way past burned vehicles. Many still smolder after the savage battle in the streets. Sparks from burning buildings are falling on us, and soon our track is set ablaze. Fortunately, we were able to put the fire out.

Enemy assault guns contest every foot of our advance. For the first time we hear the eerie sound of the screaming meemies. This, with the constant chatter of machine-gun fire, makes a very hectic night for us.

Thursday, August 17, 1944   Morning finds the situation the same, as our task force is still surrounded and cut off from the rest of the 3rd Armored Division. We have been ordered to hold our positions. There is no place for us to go, so I am sure we will be here. We have been told that all of our units have plenty of ammunition and food. Our wounded are still with us, as we have not been able to move them to the rear. Seems I have not closed my eyes for a week, afraid if I do it might be the last time.

Friday, August 18, 1944   We were elated to see large tanks of the other task force coming into this small village at dawn. When we asked why it had taken so long to reach us, one tanker said they had stopped along the way to be with the French mademoiselles.

Later, our spearheads met the British and the trap was closed. Some enemy troops escaped, but a large number were captured. In talking to some of the British and Canadian troops, we discovered they also suffered heavy losses in this battle. This conflict, in closing the Argentan–Falaise Gap, has been the most deadly and costly since we landed on Omaha Beach.

We have had no sleep for several days and rest is what we need, as everyone looks tired and haggard. Our gun crew is looking forward to a hot meal when our kitchen truck shows up. We are getting tired of eating K rations. I haven't seen Irish or Bowden for several days. Can only hope both came through this last battle OK.

Saturday, August 19, 1944   A bright, sunny day greets me as I try to relax and clean up. I'm heating water in my helmet with a blowtorch. Have not been able to shave in over a week. Did I need it? When I gazed into my broken mirror, my reflection staring back at me was like a stranger.

Sunday, August 20, 1944   We have learned by experience that all must be prepared for any emergency. Therefore everyone cleans our guns and checks out the equipment.

Monday, August 21, 1944   Two members of our gun crew are transferred to the firing batteries. Glatt and Habr have been wanting to change jobs for some time. In their place we have an Englishman whose name is Victor Doe. The other replacement is a Mexican named Escamilla. Both seem glad to be picked for our gun crew. Father makes them welcome by giving each a large drink of cognac.

Tuesday, August 22, 1944   Dawn finds us back on the dusty roads heading eastward, and all is peaceful. Our crew is fortunate to have a good driver in Otto. He never gets excited, no matter how hazardous our mission or dark the night. Just takes another chew of tobacco and then he is ready for what lies ahead.

Rumor is we are to regroup somewhere south of Paris. Night finds us still on the road, as fog settles around us. This condition adds to our hazardous journey, as we can use only blackout lights. Some of our vehicles in the convoy are lost.

Wednesday, August 23, 1944   As our convoy moves forward, we pass many smoking and charred German vehicles. Our dive-bombers have been doing a great job in preventing the enemy from retreating into Germany.

Passing through this part of France, the countryside is very pretty. Many of the roads are lined with tall trees of many different species. This would be an excellent place for us to stop and rest while taking pictures, but we are moving and I have no camera.

Thursday, August 24, 1944   The roads by day are a blur of white dust, wind, and sun, but by night they are quite a feat without lights. We take turns driving during the long nights. As the hours roll by, it seems to me like a ghost march. I'm finding that it is almost unbelievable what one can do when put to the test.

Friday, August 25, 1944   Last night our engineers constructed a bridge across the Seine River. This was accomplished in total darkness, which was no easy task. After crossing we move ahead slowly. The countryside is like Iowa in the summertime. Doc informs us he may get out of the track and wait until we come back after the war is over. It is a good idea, but it will never happen.

Saturday, August 26, 1944   Resistance is encountered soon after our spearheads branch out. Reconnaissance Company of the 33rd Armored is ambushed by a heavy enemy tank force. After being pinned down several hours, the enemy tanks are finally routed by our artillery fire supporting some of our tanks. The Germans are still in flight, for the most part. Many antiaircraft guns are being used by the enemy forces to delay our attack as we drive forward.

Although most of the action at this time does not involve as many troops as before, there is little difference. Human death is the same whether it consists of many troops or a few.

Sunday, August 27, 1944   Dawn finds us stopped in a small French village. While waiting for our convoy to move, Escamilla sees an old man lying to the side of the narrow road. We hurry over to help him, but upon examining this elderly Frenchman we find that we are too late. No doubt he had been struck by one of our tanks last night. In his worn coat was tucked a loaf of bread; we notified some French before continuing on our way. Just one more tragedy of this war.

Midday finds our spearheads crossing the Marne River. Always one more stream ahead of us. Will it ever end?

We see many Free French and find them to be a tough

and deadly organization, having fought the Germans for five years. They don't believe in taking prisoners and woe to any who fall into their clutches.

In the center of this small village we find some very excited people. With an interpreter, we learn the Free French have some collaborators surrounded in a house but no means of flushing them out of their barricade. Since we have plenty of weapons and ammunition, we very quickly give them hand grenades and other military equip- . ment. Continuing on, we hear loud explosions and the chatter of machine-gun fire. I am confident they accomplished their mission. They reward us with several tall glasses of calvados.

As night falls, we enter Château-Thierry, scene of a great battle in World War I. Now only scattered resistance is to be found. We are still moving, but much faster than when we were in Normandy.

Monday, August 28, 1944   I was awakened early by Father, who had the last watch on our gun. After he gave me a signal to be quiet, we proceeded with our guns ready to investigate an unusual noise. Creeping through the heavy weeds, we were surprised to find one of the doughs pumping water.

Today a small German convoy attempted to break through our roadblock. After a short battle, all of their vehicles were destroyed and a number of prisoners were taken.

Tuesday, August 29, 1944   On entering Braisne, units of the 486th Armored Anti-Aircraft Battalion spotted a train on the siding. Soon our forces determined it was carrying troops and tanks of our foe. Another train was located near the railroad station, too. The following battle was deadly and savage. Some of the enemy troops manned the heavy tanks on the flatcars. The firepower of our artillery was used in this attack. In the end, many of the German tanks were destroyed, and all of the enemy who chose to surrender were taken prisoner. As is always the case, we suffered losses in this engagement, too. Both trains were left burning at the end of this conflict. Later some enemy planes dropped flares on us and a church was set ablaze, which cast an eerie glow over the entire town.

It was a very busy and noisy night for all, and we were glad to see morning come. We crossed the Aisne River bridge, which was secured intact.

Wednesday, August 30, 1944   Morning finds our task forces moving forward very slowly. The terrain here is hilly and heavily wooded. This area must be scouted very thoroughly before we can proceed. The 83rd Reconnaissance Battalion is suffering losses in their probing attacks through this area. We are being continuously fired upon by snipers. We received orders to spray the wooded hillsides with our machine guns. This is proving to be an effective means of reducing our casualties. We managed to flush out one sniper near dusk.

Thursday, August 31, 1944   Our crew has a roadblock set up at the edge of a small village. A platoon of infantry has dug in with us.

As we were getting ready to eat our cold meal, we had some excitement instead. Five Germans in a large command car tried to crash through our lines. Turned out to be a suicide attempt on their part, as they never made it through. After this short encounter, we had no prisoners to guard.

Friday, September 1, 1944   Clouds of fine dust mark the route of our spearhead columns as we near Belgium. Our destination has been changed and we are driving north. Our task forces are encountering only delaying action by the enemy — mostly roadblocks and sniper fire.

Doe takes over driving for Otto, as our driver is exhausted from the countless miles of travel. Maintaining position in a convoy is a very hectic job, especially at night using only blackout lights. Our forces are moving out of the flat country into some rolling hills. The countryside is very pretty along our route.

Saturday, September 2, 1944   We drove across the border into Belgium this morning. Everywhere I look I see wild, shouting people who scream greetings to us. Flowers are everywhere on our route of advance, and our vehicles are soon covered with all colors of bouquets. Again many bottles of beverages are thrust into our eager hands.

After several short conflicts, the high ground west of Mons has been taken. As darkness falls, all enemy resistance has ceased and our forces occupy all of the city.

4
The Surprise Battle

By the time the 3rd Armored Division reached Mons on September 2, it had outpaced mixed columns of about 30,000 retreating German troops and vehicles from various units. It now turned to face them to cut off their retreat to the relative safety of the Siegfried Line farther east. On September 3, Willis's gun crew set up a roadblock west of Mons and demonstrated their effectiveness against one of these columns, an infantry column unsupported by tanks.

With the death or capture of thousands of additional troops at Mons, the German army was even weaker and more disorganized than it had been. At this time it could have offered little resistance to a single, determined Allied thrust into Germany. But, for a number of reasons, the Allies did not make such a thrust. Montgomery's 21st Army Group took Brussels on September 3 and Antwerp on September 4 but then settled in to prepare for the now famous assault on the five Dutch bridges ending at Arnhem. Patton's Third Army ground to a halt before Metz, south of the Ardennes. Between them, the U.S. First Army (to which the 3rd Armored Division was assigned) was channeled along a narrow corridor through central Belgium between Brussels and the Ardennes to cover Montgomery's right flank, and Willis chronicled their progress through Belgium in his diary.

Sunday, September 3, 1944   I was awakened early this morning to the familiar sound of gunfire. After a hurried breakfast of cold K rations, our gun crew is ordered to report to one of our officers. We soon learn our division is in a very perilous position. An entire German army is attempting to break through our lines on their retreat back to Germany.

Quickly we are ordered to set up a roadblock several miles west of Mons. Upon arriving there in the early morning hours, we find no one else is in the vicinity. Our crew spends some time digging in our antitank gun behind a small rise. Father sets up his .30-calibre machine gun behind a large tree, Otto backs our track to a fortified position near a small house, and I climb into our iron machine by my gun turret. I check my ammunition belts and place extra barrels close to my machine gun. Although we can hear sounds of battle, it seems to be several miles away. However, clouds of dust are observed on the road in the direction our guns are pointing.

Over the skyline, troops who appear to be marching in parade move toward our roadblock. Doe remarks, "Those troops must be prisoners of war on the way back to a collecting point." By now Father's curiosity has caused him to run over to our track. After locating his field glasses, he returns to where we are standing. He takes a long look to the west at the oncoming troops. Quickly he hands his glasses to Stack, and our gunner loses no time in returning them. He informs us of the situation with one word, "Germans." We need no urging, as all know that our only chance to survive is to surprise the enemy. Seconds later, at Stack's signal, both machine guns, along with our 57 mm antitank gun, are spreading death and destruction among the advancing German forces. Very soon our crew, using armor-piercing shells, has disabled the enemy gun and blown up the track pulling it. We continue to direct explosive fire upon the German forces.

Father and I decide to take turns firing. By this method we have time to change barrels on our guns when they become too hot to operate. This battle is by no means one-sided. Angry bullets are whistling all around us. Stack and the rest of his crew are forced to leave their gun, which is in an exposed position. All are dug in near our machine guns for a stand.

As the long day progresses we realize more troops are needed to hold our roadblock, as there are only six men in our crew. Three times during this long, hot September day we send for help, but no one arrives until late in the evening.

As the sun is setting in the west, we are overjoyed to

hear the Germans yelling "Kamerad!" Father and I, with
the remainder of our crew covering us with machine guns,
go forward to accept their surrender. Father always seems
to think I want to do everything he does. This is not always
true. Nevertheless, I go along with him and together we
capture some enemy troops. A short time later, more of our
troops arrive on the scene as the remainder of the German
troops surrender to our force.

The German survivors can hardly believe that our
crew consists of only six soldiers.

Monday, September 4, 1944   We learned that in the
battle at Mons our division captured thousands of Germans in spite of being greatly outnumbered. Many would
not surrender and were eliminated on the battlefield. Our
P-47 Thunderbolts were a great help to our forces in
stopping the enemy armor. The 3rd Armored Division was
very fortunate in being able to turn the tide of battle into a
victory.

I'm trying to relax some after yesterday, which was a
very, very long day. I've been looking for a button to sew on
my field jacket that an enemy sharpshooter clipped off my
shoulder during the battle. My luck is still holding, but
that bullet was close.

The 1st Infantry Division is taking over here as we
prepare to move on toward Germany. Cheering Belgians
mob our convoy as we advance through the narrow streets
of Mons. Tanks and trucks are loaded with happy girls and
children. There is joy everywhere and a number of moist
eyes, also.

Tuesday, September 5, 1944   Moved forward during
the night after leaving Mons. We received heavy shellfire
from the enemy artillery. A friend of mine was killed last
night. He was married before leaving the States but will
never see his daughter.

Our forces discover a bridge intact at Namur. To help
speed our crossing, our engineers build another one to
cross the Meuse River.

Wednesday, September 6, 1944   As our spearheads move forward, we receive harassing fire from small groups of enemy defenders. We have set up our roadblock on the edge of Liège overlooking the approaches to the city.

This morning I have the good fortune to meet two very kind Belgian civilians — an old man and his pretty granddaughter. They insist, in broken English, that I accompany them to their home. I am treated to fresh bread and milk. I also learn that the rest of their family is in concentration camps in Germany. With their blessings ringing in my ears, I return to my buddies across the street. I will never forget their kindness.

We encounter snipers in the area. Although only one tank destroyer soldier was killed at this time, it was the method used which enraged all of us. He was found with his towel and soap still in his hand, and his pockets had been rifled. This tanker had been shot in the head. With all helping in the search, we soon rounded up the snipers. They never caused any more trouble.

During the night our crew captured a German captain, who seemed happy to surrender. I've got his watch and P-38 pistol for safekeeping. All stay awake the rest of the night, as the enemy is everywhere.

Thursday, September 7, 1944   As our columns drive through Liège this morning, we find a city of happiness. The welcome is greater than those received in France. The city is practically undamaged, and the Belgian population is wild with joy as our spearhead tanks rumble over the wide cobblestone avenues.

Everywhere people are dancing in the streets and riding on our tanks and other vehicles. Once again, cognac flows and pretty girls overwhelm us. We receive kisses, flowers, gifts, and even ice cream. This makes only twice we have had ice cream in over a year.

For a fleeting moment, my thoughts go back to America, where people are safe. How much we take for granted — the good life. I hope we never have in our country what these people here in Europe have experienced in past years. When evening draws near, we leave these happy people of Liège. As we cross the river to the east side, I see several Jerry planes in the sky, but they make no move to delay us.

Friday, September 8, 1944   After traveling most of the night, dawn finds our convoy stopped on the road. While night slowly fades away, we observe a large tank near a small house. Peering through the hazy half-light, we pay very little attention at first to this scene. But as the day becomes lighter, we are startled to see that this tank looks very much like a German tank. Deciding to investigate, we arm and very quickly slip quietly closer to find that indeed it is an enemy tank. By now we have been joined by more of our troops. Together we surround the small house. The German tank crew was very surprised when roughly awakened by our soldiers. After taking them prisoner, we toss a couple of thermal grenades down the barrel of the gun on their tank.

We move into the city of Verviers. Many of the people speak English, which is a welcome sound to us. Again we are slowed by celebrating Belgians, who give us a joyous greeting. Would be nice to linger here for a while, but I know this is not to be.

Saturday, September 9, 1944   Our P-47 Thunderbolts are still with us, as the weather is nice with clear skies. Our spearheads are still advancing on all roads. I see our planes diving and strafing ahead of our column. Only scattered opposition is encountered.

We are near a farmhouse this morning and have our gun set up by a pile of rocks. The owner has given me three pictures for souvenirs. One is a photograph of his home. On one picture he has written these words: "Souvener de Belgigne a 20 KM de la ligne Siegfried. Henri Gaby, Digon, Belgigne." Translated they mean, "Souvenir of Belgium, 20 kilometers from the Siegfried Line." Signed by this farmer.

We entered a small Belgian village near dusk. We were startled to see the bodies of two men and a woman hanging from a large awning over an inn. This gruesome sight was very quickly removed. This terrible crime was no doubt a reprisal against these people.

Sunday, September 10, 1944   As morning comes, we are once again on the roads with the task force. Near noon our dive-bombers can be seen blasting enemy tanks. At this time we are getting very close to Germany. Resistance is stronger now, as there are numerous roadblocks and blown bridges ahead. Many new enemy units are observed by our task forces.

5
Through the Siegfried Line

By September 11, 1944, the 3rd Armored Division had pushed rapidly eastward to the fortified line the Allies called the Siegfried Line, though the official German name for it was the Westwall. By whatever name, the Allied commanders had enormous respect for it as a defensive position. Because of the significance of the sector for the Germans, they had, in fact, built two defensive lines to protect the cities of Aachen and Stolberg. The lighter defensive network, the Scharnhorst Line, was located just west of Aachen, while a more elaborate system, the Schill Line (which Willis calls "the Second Siegfried Line"), lay west of Stolberg. Both lines extended on into the Huertgen Forest to the south.

Surprisingly, the initial thrust against the German defenses met only modest resistance from the network of pillboxes once the American tanks had overcome the antitank obstacle of cement pyramids known as "dragon's teeth." The reason for this was that the losses the German forces had taken throughout the summer, and most recently at Mons, left them with very little equipment and very few troops (and these of poor quality) to man the elaborate defensive network. As a result, Willis's early diary entries record a sense of relief and pride that the American forces led by the 3rd Armored Division had cracked the Siegfried Line and were on German soil by September 15.

The Germans were quickly able to scrape together a sufficient force to halt the American thrust, however, and in fact to bring to a near standstill the rapid triumphal march that had begun on the Seine far back in France. As Willis's later entries record, fighting in the sector around Stolberg, Aachen, and the Huertgen Forest turned into a bloody slugfest, with the overextended American forces making only very slow progress against the German defenses and the Germans initiating seemingly endless local counterattacks. The 3rd Armored Division was in reserve through most of this fighting, though Willis's reassignment in late September to a gun crew assigned to defend the division's headquarters company placed him close enough to the front to witness the American progress, or lack of it.

Monday, September 11, 1944   Daylight finds our armored columns moving through the border town of Eupen. Very few victory signs or flowers are seen. Only hate-filled faces stare at us from windows and doorways. All sense our cheerful welcomes are coming to a very quick end. From now on we must be on guard against the civilians, too.

The gates of Germany loom before our forces. Dirty, ragged, and with our nerves screaming from lack of sleep plus the constant concussion of guns ringing in our ears, we prepare to begin the assault on the Siegfried Line.

Tuesday, September 12, 1944   The Siegfried Line (the Westwall of Germany) we have heard so much about lies directly ahead. A maze of forts fortified with heavy guns has been built into the terrain of hills and valleys. They look ominous and foreboding before us.

We see the dragon's teeth — cement barricades which cannot be moved except by explosives. All sense something terrifying is confronting us. The massive fortifications directly in front of our division are going to be very difficult to penetrate. To add to the problems facing our forces, the weather has turned foul and all the planes are grounded.

Although our infantry has secured high ground beyond the dragon's teeth, they have stopped until our tanks can catch up with them. Our engineers are called upon to blow a hole through the cement barricades. This operation is finally accomplished, but all the while under heavy fire from German forts. Our Sherman tanks, with flails attached to detonate enemy mines, move forward. Many loud explosions fill the air as the numerous deadly mines are tripped by this maneuver. This operation is followed by more tanks using dozers which smooth their route.

Every means available is being used to break through this heavily fortified German line of defense at the Siegfried Line. As our line of attack unfolds, our forces are constantly being supported by the artillery batteries' many thundering guns. Our tanks and infantry forces move

forward through a murderous hail of machine-gun and
small-arms fire. Mortar bursts are everywhere as slowly we
creep into the heavy defense.

Night comes and the savage battle continues without
pause. It seems to me as if an inferno must be close by as
the grim toll of dead mounts hour by hour. When possible,
our medics bring out the wounded, but many times
during this long night it is hopelessly difficult. The cost is
high in men and machines as the hours drag by. There is
no sleep for any among our troops. A great deal of blood is
spilled before the crack of dawn.

Wednesday, September 13, 1944   As morning comes
we receive orders for our crew to set up our gun near a
fortified pillbox. Upon arriving at our destination, we find
a platoon of infantry waiting for us. In talking with them,
we learn that many of our units suffered heavy losses from
last night's battle.

We receive more startling news. The fort we have our
gun near is still occupied by German troops. Soon several
155 mm self-propelled artillery guns move up close to the
enemy fort. They spend some time firing directly at the
massive pillbox but have no success. Finally, our engineers
are called upon to devise a plan. They are now welding the
iron trapdoors shut, thus sealing the Germans inside
their bunkers. This strategy should give the enemy time to
think about surrendering!

We have moved to the edge of a small town which is
near Aachen. Our antitank gun is set up with a fortified
machine-gun nest. No time to rest, as the enemy forces are
still counterattacking everywhere.

As night comes, I see many tanks burning, with black
smoke drifting into the sky. Another hectic night for all as
the bright flash of heavy guns lights up the terrain around
us. Our troops have been able to hold the ground we
occupy, but barely.

Thursday, September 14, 1944   The second Siegfried

Line is cleared to Stolberg. Many burned-out tanks dot the landscape. Very few Germans are seen around here. Most must have moved back into Germany before we arrived.

Our location is near large forests. The rainy weather is still with us, and we cannot count on any help from our planes. Our crew is now eating at the kitchen truck again. We have had about one hot meal every two weeks lately.

Friday, September 15, 1944   We are living in luxury on the edge of Germany. We were lucky to be able to move into a hotel. Don't know the price of our rooms, as no one is here to collect the rent.

Our antitank gun is set up in front of our quarters, while the ammunition train is bivouacked some distance away in a meadow. Heavy mortar fire is received from the enemy. Today we learned that our division is the first to crack the Siegfried Line. This was accomplished in spite of foul weather and with no air support. The operation was very costly to our forces.

Saturday, September 16, 1944   Another day finds our crew still staying in the nice sleeping quarters of this hotel. The few Germans around are very well dressed and are causing no problems for us.

After dinner we checked out some German barracks at the edge of a large forest. We found them to have deep air-raid shelters nearby. Also located quite a number of souvenirs in our search.

It is fortunate for us that Father had laid in a generous supply of cognac before our arrival in Germany. No one has offered us anything except trouble in this country.

Sunday, September 17, 1944   I was beginning to enjoy this Sabbath when I learned we had to vacate our luxury hotel. Our major moved our gun crew forward about a mile to the center of a forest. We are in the company of eight tanks and have been told our forces are expecting a counterattack soon. Cannot dig holes for shelter, as the trees are too close together.

We have chalked up an amazing record. The 3rd Armored Division drove from the Seine River to the Siegfried Line in eighteen days. The trip was a long, hard road for all of us. Everyone looks haggard from fatigue as we pause to catch our breath. Our division must have replacements and supplies to continue our drive.

Monday, September 18, 1944   The enemy launched another heavy attack during the night hours. No sleep tonight, as we have to stay alert. I'm going to try getting a few hours of rest today if I can find the time. No chance of relaxing when we are under siege by the Germans. This area is so damp we cannot find any dry wood. A fire would probably be seen by the enemy and result in more shelling.

The tankers with us are sure good company, and the guns on their tanks are much larger than ours. They are also used to being alone. They were sure surprised to find we had so much cognac with us. However, after meeting Father I'm certain they understood the reason we have plenty of beverages. We have been low on food a few times, but never on drinks.

Tuesday, September 19, 1944   It is raining very heavily and will be sort of foggy when it does stop for awhile. The thick trees seem to help screen us from the water. Most of the time we get under our track. It is as safe as anywhere, except for a direct hit. I try to avoid thinking of this happening.

Our quarters at the nice hotel were much better than where we are now bivouacked. Everyone on our crew has been griping since we had to move.

Wednesday, September 20, 1944   We are confronted with still another menace. Sniper fire has been received throughout the forest. Spent a good part of the day trying to locate where it is coming from, but have had no success in our search.

I'm trying to keep a low profile as much as I can. Our division is still attacking and trying to capture Stolberg, as we are now at the edge of the city. It is mostly an infantry operation supported by artillery and tanks. Our forces are in the process of trying to establish a stable front line.

Thursday, September 21, 1944   We were awakened very early this morning by heavy enemy shellfire. A gas truck was hit near our area and very soon became a roaring inferno. This development gave the enemy an extra target on which to zero their guns.

Received orders to pull our forces back to the barracks this evening. It is much nicer here, as we at least have a roof over us when it storms. We are closer to our battery, so may get a hot meal from the kitchen truck. I'm looking forward to some much-needed rest.

Received a paper from the United States government telling us not to fraternize with the Germans.

Friday, September 22, 1944   The tanks with their crews left our area this morning. They had received orders for another mission. We were sorry to see them go, as they were good company and their large tanks made us feel more secure. Father gave them a merry departure by loading their tanks with cognac. There is a forward observer crew with us now.

Found some air-raid shelters close by. This discovery will save us some labor in hole digging. The ground is covered with mushrooms. We have been busy gathering them in our steel helmets. A delicious meal was enjoyed this evening. Such a welcome change from our rations.

Saturday, September 23, 1944   Stack informs his crew to move into a small house near the barracks. This is good news, as we will still be close to the air-raid shelters. However, we are still quite a distance from our battery.

After several days of heavy fighting, our forces now occupy half of the city of Stolberg. The 1st Infantry

Division has been holding at the front. The 3rd Armored Division is now regrouping and taking stock of our losses. It is beginning to look like the American army has ground to a halt just inside Germany.

Sunday, September 24, 1944   Last night brought a new attack by the enemy. With the support of our artillery batteries, our forces were able to contain them. A few Jerries were over also during the night dropping flares and bombs, but did very little damage in our sector. A lone enemy plane flies over each evening at midnight. We have nicknamed him "Bed-Check Charlie." Disappointment looms when he fails to appear.

After receiving orders forbidding all troops to fraternize with the enemy, some are paying no heed. One of our buddies had been seeing a girl in Stolberg the past few days. When he failed to appear at his post, a search party was sent out. Later an infantry patrol found him in an alley with a knife in his back. No one is seeing any fräuleins in Stolberg now.

Monday, September 25, 1944   More German artillery shells are coming into our area every day. The Krauts must have received a new supply of ammunition. Aside from shellfire, air raids, and patrol action, all is quiet here at the front. The only moving we do is in our own area.

We have been getting a few clear days which bring out our planes to harass the enemy positions. But for the most part it has been rain and mud. The weather has proven to be an obstacle to our tanks and other vehicles. It has certainly given our infantry even worse living conditions at the front.

Tuesday, September 26, 1944   The hotel which our crew occupied for a few days was destroyed by a bomb last night. Lt. Stewart and Sgt. Kyauski, sleeping upstairs, were killed. Several other members of the ammunition train were wounded. A friend of mine named Maxwell may lose his arm and no doubt will be sent home. Irish was also sleeping at the hotel but was lucky, as he received only minor cuts.

Wednesday, September 27, 1944   We are being constantly subjected to heavy artillery and mortar fire. The attacks are increasing and many of their guns are on railroad cars. The shells leave deep holes in the earth. Our maintenance battalion was hit very heavy from their fire a few days ago.

I see several German civilians working in their fields. They never seem to be hit by shellfire; must have camouflaged shelters near.

Thursday, September 28, 1944   Father and I received orders that we have been transferred to the other antitank gun. Now we are part of Headquarters. The brass decided that they needed more protection, and we are picked for the job. We find that our gun is closer to the action.

An ex-barber by the name of Sam Danton is our new gunner. Liwo, the first loader, is from Detroit, and the second loader is Spillman, whose home state is Kentucky. Farr, our driver, comes from South Carolina.

Friday, September 29, 1944   The Jerries were out again last night. During their bombing attack, one of our M7 105 mm self-propelled guns was destroyed. Nearly all of the crew were lost. Another sleepless night, as they gave us a rough time. It was as if they had their targets marked.

Farr found a stray dog and named him Fritz. He is at home with us. Of course, the food is good and his ration comes first. Our driver has been digging him a shelter, too, and is training Fritz to use it.

Saturday, September 30, 1944   Had another close shave this morning. Was in a dugout with part of my crew when a flying boxcar came in. Caved in one side of our shelter. No one was injured, just shaken up some.

Liwo has located several gardens. He is fond of fried potatoes, so he has been busy getting his winter's supply. Sure has found a good method of obtaining them. Just pulls out the spuds, leaving the vines undisturbed. He told us he would like to see the Germans when they return to harvest their crop. He is in possession of the largest frying pan I have ever seen. No doubt he liberated this cooking utensil somewhere along our route. However, this member of our crew does not believe in sharing with us.

Sunday, October 1, 1944   We suffered another heavy bombing raid last night. Didn't receive much damage in our sector, though. Air attacks are increasing. I dread every night, as we cannot get very much rest.

Farr's dog has become a good lookout for us. Can smell Germans and gives us a warning when they are near. He has a keen sense of hearing, also, and can detect incoming shells before we hear them. When we observe him jumping into his shelter, we know it is time for us to move.

Monday, October 2, 1944   As usual, the sky was filled with German planes last night. They got a surprise as our ack-ack guns opened up on them. Several of their planes went down in flames. All were happy to see their attacks opposed by our forces. We seldom see the Luftwaffe during the day.

Tuesday, October 3, 1944   Today is my birthday, but I doubt if I get a cake. I sure hope to be home next year. I am not enjoying where I am, but I'm still among the living, for which I am very thankful. I'm surprised we have not moved before now. We usually don't stay in one place very long.

I managed to get a good night's sleep for a change. Everyone was bushed, including me. It is very quiet around here today, too much so. Something is in the wind. We will pay for it later.

Wednesday, October 4, 1944   Another dull day in Germany finds me writing a few letters and just taking life easy. What a welcome change when we are fortunate to have a few hours of quiet. Just finished taking a bath in my steel helmet. Our plumbing isn't too modern, so we just have to make do with what is available.

The USO girls gave a show in Stolberg. Marlene Dietrich was among them. She is an actress from Hollywood. They have lots of nerve getting this close to the front. I was able to attend, as one of my buddies pulled my turn at guard on our gun.

Thursday, October 5, 1944   Awoke to find the sun still shines in Germany occasionally. Several P-47 Thunderbolts are in the sky above our position. Upon counting, I find their force is sixteen bombers. As they dive upon the enemy lines I am reminded of swallows zooming around our barn on the farm back home. But it is only a reminder, as their flaming guns followed by loud explosions from the bombs bring my thoughts back to reality.

As we watch this drama unfold in the sky, one of our planes does not come out of the dive. We observe a large ball of flames, which is followed by heavy black smoke. One more name is added to the long list of American dead.

Friday, October 6, 1944   Today, we learn a large panzer division consisting of many tanks is trying to recapture our sector of Stolberg. Not much chance, as the veteran 1st Infantry Division is here with us.

We are falling into the same old routine each day. Have no idea when we will be moving again. It is much different than when we were traveling through France and Belgium. Sometimes I begin feeling sorry for myself, but then I think of the infantry on the front line all of the time. Soon I realize I am fortunate in comparison to the life they are leading.

Saturday, October 7, 1944   Another clear day as I rise

to meet the elements. I was lucky to see another USO show. Some of the boys didn't care to go. The girls put on a good performance and the price was right. The poor civilians back in the States have to pay for their entertainment.

Not much action around here today, and that is the way it should be all the time. I find that we are running low on beverages. Father is having to scout much farther in his search. He still manages to return with his arms full of bottles.

Sunday, October 8, 1944   Our gun crew received orders this morning to move closer to the front. Spillman remarked that he was surprised that we had not been moved before.

We are busy most of the day digging in our gun. The Krauts are probably having a good laugh watching us. The ground here is a mixture of rock and shale, with tree roots mixed in. This proves to be quite a task to fortify our position.

Monday, October 9, 1944   German artillery shelled our area most of the day. Must have observed us yesterday when we were setting up our antitank gun. We were lucky to find a cave near, which we used for shelter during the heaviest enemy firing.

Farr's dog, Fritz, alerted us just before the shells arrived. He is sure a valuable dog to have around.

Tuesday, October 10, 1944   Our officers finally decided we had been spotted by the foe. We have orders to move from this hill down into a valley. There is a large factory here, which we are using for sleeping quarters. Part of our maintenance battalion is with us. Their officer, Captain Lee, is in charge of all the troops in this area. Our crew is sure glad to be in out of the weather. We have been playing poker in the evening when not on guard.

Wednesday, October 11, 1944   All troops have been

informed once more not to associate with the Germans. Nearly all of the civilians are women and children. I notice some of the women are getting friendlier as the days go by. Captain Lee doesn't care what we do when off guard. However, I can't forget our buddy who was found in Stolberg with a knife in his back. I don't intend to be very friendly with the enemy.

Thursday, October 12, 1944   Enemy planes dropped a load of antipersonnel bombs in back of the factory where we are located. No noticeable damage, but it forced us to leave our poker game and seek shelter.

Father was asleep in his new bedroll and couldn't get out, as the zipper stuck. Some of us had to return to the factory to assist him. He had been drinking quite heavily, which added to the confusion. Everything turned out fine, as no one was injured.

Friday, October 13, 1944   A German robot passed over our area this evening on its mission of destruction. A few minutes later we saw it again in the sky heading east. Adolph will be surprised to receive it back.

We are entering into an unusually wet season again. Sticky clay clings to all of the vehicles. It is a hard task keeping all equipment clean and in smooth operating condition.

At least we are still in out of the weather part of the time. The infantry has far worse living conditions, especially up in the desolated Huertgen Forest, due to the heavy shelling. Much of the terrain resembles the battlefields of World War I.

Saturday, October 14, 1944   I hitched a ride back to the ammunition train to see Irish. He told me they had been getting some heavy shelling. Again I invited him to come up to the front and see some real action. He didn't seem too eager to return with me. They have been busier than usual hauling shells to the firing batteries. It is beginning to look as if we are being prepared for another drive.

Sunday, October 15, 1944   This morning a large shell landed near a friend of mine; there were no dog tags to mail home. We see more action on the front every day. We are, however, pretty comfortable at our quarters in this old factory. Each evening sees a big poker game, which is relaxing. I'm nearly rested from the long drive from Normandy.

Monday, October 16, 1944   Received half a dozen letters from home today. Answered most of them this evening, as we have more idle time now.

Yes! We have electric lights here in the factory. Maintenance hooked up some wires to their truck generator. Still have to keep all windows covered, though. All the comforts of home! That statement is not quite true. Time seems to be dragging again as we await new orders.

Tuesday, October 17, 1944   Aachen is surrounded by our troops. They have been given an ultimatum to surrender. It will be suicide if they choose to fight. The sky is clear and our planes will be able to assist us.

This evening our officers receive news that the German mans will defend the city of Aachen. Many lives will be lost on both sides by their decision. As darkness comes, the roar of many tanks is heard as our forces move forward for the assault upon this stronghold.

Wednesday, October 18, 1944   With the coming of dawn, the battle for Aachen begins. The firing batteries roar as salvo after salvo of shells rains death and destruction upon the city. The 1st Infantry leads the attack, supported by tanks and large guns.

From where I stand I see scores of our dive-bombers supporting the attack. Darting down and out, they seem like angry bees as they continue to bomb and strafe throughout the long day. Many buildings are set ablaze, throwing large clouds of black smoke over the city. Still, in spite of this rain of destruction, the infantry and tanks are meeting heavy resistance as they drive forward to secure the ground. The assault forces are suffering heavy losses.

Thursday, October 19, 1944   The city of Aachen fell to our forces today. It was a scene of destruction as we rode down the wide avenues. We see the all-too-familiar sight of smoking ruins that were once a proud and beautiful city. This is the first large German city to fall to our forces. I am sure many more will follow.

The infantry has liberated quite a few cases of cognac. No doubt Father will find some way to replenish our supply, which is running low.

Friday, October 20, 1944   We heard that a few passes will be given to cities of France and Belgium. I'm not too interested, so have not looked into the matter. Only a few of the troops will be able to leave.

The front is fairly quiet today. Only a few shells coming in once in a while. The maintenance battalion is very busy working on all equipment. It must be in good condition when we move on. All the tanks are being reinforced with heavy iron plating and sandbags. We could have used some of this heavier protection going through the Siegfried Line.

Saturday, October 21, 1944   Another lazy day greets me as I crawl out of my bedroll. The weather reminds me of Indian summer back in Iowa. It seems years since we came ashore in Normandy, although the time has been only a few short months. Some days seem like a lifetime.

This afternoon I finally convinced our ex-barber that I needed a haircut. Sure did look shaggy, and a shampoo wouldn't hurt my appearance. He will not cut anyone's hair unless he is in a good mood, which isn't very often.

Sunday, October 22, 1944   Received word today that our ammunition train was bombed by the enemy during the night. One of my buddies was wounded again. Dan was in the hotel when it was destroyed a few weeks ago. Doubt if he returns this time. I used to write letters for him, as he had no education.

Monday, October 23, 1944   We are not getting any rest tonight, as the Luftwaffe is over our positions to harass us with their bombing raids. Beginning at midnight, the sky is soon bright with countless flares. Soon large fires are burning from the hits scored by the enemy planes. This action by the Jerries is so frequent that I dread every night.

Tuesday, October 24, 1944   Several of us got a patrol together and spent several hours exploring parts of the Siegfried Line. We found pillboxes that range in thickness from four to eight feet of reinforced concrete. Added to this defense are many guns of various sizes, which are now disabled.

The deadly 88 mm is found to be their main heavy gun. All pillboxes have modern living quarters which are self-contained, with supplies and ammunition. Many air vents and fans kept fresh air circulating into the rooms. After examining these German fortress defenses, I understand the reason it was so difficult to break through the Siegfried Line.

Wednesday, October 25, 1944   Our gun crew, who weren't on guard, took a trip into Stolberg. Managed to locate some beer, but it wasn't too good. We will have to drink cognac when we are thirsty.

Gazing around, I come to the conclusion that our division must move before long or else there will be no shelter for anyone. This area is slowly but surely being reduced to rubble.

Thursday, October 26, 1944   Received extra greetings

from the Germans this morning. A Flying Boxcar came in
early; must have been from railroad guns. Could barely
hear them cough in the distance, then it seemed forever
before they arrived. But when the barrage reached its
destination, it made up for the delay. The destructive
power of these enormous shells is almost unbelievable.
The heavy explosives create holes in which a tank could be
buried. The enemy zeroed in on our armored maintenance
battalion a few miles to the rear of us. Some of our troops
were hit by shrapnel in this shelling. There is very little
protection from the fire of these large guns.

Friday, October 27, 1944   Another day, another dollar!
I wonder if I am earning mine. Sure glad to have a roof over
us, as the rainy season is coming.

More replacements have arrived. The fields around
here are full of equipment and supplies. The supply
battalion has been very busy making long trips to the rear.
They have been harassed by isolated pockets of the foe.

We will have to move soon, as Liwo is running low on
his supply of potatoes. He has cleaned out all of the
gardens in this vicinity but still will not share with his
crew.

Saturday, October 28, 1944   We are still waiting for
our orders. It certainly seems that we have been in Germany for a long, long time, while in reality it has been only
a few weeks.

I'm ready for this war to end so we can return home.

Sunday, October 29, 1944   Took time today to write a
letter home to Steve Stevenson, the editor of the local
paper. I doubt if the strikers or P.W. will like the story. In it I
wrote that the people who are complaining for more
should have a tour of duty over here. They would very soon
be singing a different tune.

Also, have been hearing how well the P.W. are being
treated in the States. Perhaps we should not have cap-

tured such large numbers of them. Would have saved much trouble and expense.

Monday, October 30, 1944   The news this morning is not good. The ammunition is now rationed for our firing batteries. This will have a negative effect on the infantry at the front. They certainly need all of the firepower our artillery can supply.

The weather is getting much colder, especially at night. Winter is getting much closer, and I am not too happy with this event. When the ground freezes we will not be able to dig shelters for protection. Looking ahead, the future is dismal.

Tuesday, October 31, 1944   The Germans must have been informed that our ammunition was rationed. They opened up an attack all along the front this morning. It was preceded by a very heavy mortar barrage. Their heavy armor, with infantry support, moved forward. Our firing batteries couldn't do much firing due to being rationed. However, some heavy artillery which is attached to our division soon stopped the enemy assault. Due to the continuing foul weather, we get no help from our planes.

Each passing day our sector is looking more like World War I. The days drag along and it seems to me I have been here forever. Cannot relax or trust the civilians. Have to be looking over our shoulders all of the time.

Wednesday, November 1, 1944   All signs around here look as if there will be another big push soon. Convoys of supplies and replacement troops continue to arrive. Now every abandoned house is being used as shelter for our troops. All of our equipment which is worn out or has been lost is being replaced by new. This tells me something is in the wind. At least we will be ready when the next drive comes.

The armored maintenance battalion is working twenty-four hours a day repairing all tanks and other vehicles.

Many of the tanks are being equipped with large rollers in front to detonate minefields.

While our forces have been stopped, the enemy has been very busy fortifying their defense lines. When we move ahead the road will be rough and very dangerous.

Thursday, November 2, 1944   The weather is rainy and is getting colder each day. Still have no means of heating our quarters in the factory. Winter is close and I am not looking forward to enjoying it. However, we may not be here when the snow comes.

It is too rainy and muddy for Liwo to dig potatoes, even if a garden could be found. Our supply of mushrooms has been eaten long ago. So we will have to eat K rations or find our kitchen truck.

Friday, November 3, 1944   Several of us went on a hazardous hunt all day. We have been receiving sniper fire again in our area for several days. Finally decided to get a patrol together and see what we could uncover. Although we searched most of the day, our efforts were in vain. No one is in a good mood when a sniper is found. Too many Americans have been slain by them along the roads from Omaha Beach.

Farr still has his watchdog, Fritz, with him. Sleeps in a bedroll at night, really has a good life-style. Our driver plans on taking him back to South Carolina when he returns home.

Saturday, November 4, 1944   A clear day as Indian summer lingers. Some of our dive-bombers are out to harass the enemy lines. We observed a P-47 Thunderbolt crash in flames; he never had a chance to bail out. Probably would not have done any good anyway. German antiaircraft would have hit him before he reached the ground. The Krauts have no respect for our pilots.

Sunday, November 5, 1944   Played poker with some of

my buddies this evening. I was very lucky, as my share of
the winnings was over one hundred dollars. Cannot send
it home, as we are restricted on the amount we mail back
to the States each month. Doesn't make sense to me, but
that is the rule. Most all of the troops like to play cards.
Anyway, it keeps my mind off other things. Have very little
recreation around this part of Germany. Ended up my
evening writing a couple of letters home.

Monday, November 6, 1944   Another sleepless night,
as the enemy attacked along our line again. As usual, we
received very heavy shellfire. Machine-gun bullets ripped
through our quarters. Was lucky, as no one was hit. Tried
to find the source but had no success. May have been
indirect firing by the enemy while they were attacking.

Tuesday, November 7, 1944   Morning still finds the
enemy counterattacking our forces. Clear skies bring out
our planes in record numbers. They sure look good to us
up there in the blue. Today their bombs destroyed many
large German tanks, with black smoke and flame marking
the site of the hits. By late afternoon the attack had
stopped and the enemy had been thrown back.

Wednesday, November 8, 1944   The Germans are
active again with their field guns. Shellfire is increasing as
we gear up for the coming battles. Although their shelling
isn't doing much damage, it is hard on my nerves and
keeps one from getting much rest. Their barrages are so
frequent I don't venture far from shelter. The enemy has
plenty of ammunition for all of his guns.

Thursday, November 9, 1944   Still not much going on
in our sector of the front. I wrote a couple of letters, since
I've plenty of time now. Sure is quiet around here this
evening; one could almost forget where we are. Hope to get
a good night of rest for a change.

Near midnight, Farr and his watchdog check the

factory to make certain all is secure. They have appointed themselves extra security guards. They are usually the last to hit the sack. We are fortunate to have Fritz around.

Friday, November 10, 1944   A couple of buddies and I drove back to the rear area in a peep. While on the trip, one of our Flying Fortress planes accidentally dropped a heavy bomb near us. Gave us an added scare, as we are not used to bombs from friendly planes.

We had not been back this far from the front for some time. Was surprised to find all villages and fields crowded with new equipment. Our division is near full strength. A record number of replacements have arrived.

The German civilians are very busy cleaning up their towns and resuming their lives. Most shops are open, and many homes are once again occupied.

Saturday, November 11, 1944   Armistice Day! It doesn't make much difference to us. No doubt someone forgot to inform us to stop for a few minutes around eleven o'clock. When going to school, we would pause for awhile on this day. Now that is only a memory to us. Will the world ever learn? What a price to pay.

Sunday, November 12, 1944   Rumors are out again of another big drive coming soon. Hope our good weather continues, as we will need all the help we can get. Our fighter-bombers are often the difference between victory and defeat. All cannot praise them enough for their dangerous mission of helping our forces.

Monday, November 13, 1944   The ground is sticky ribbons of mud. The past few weeks of heavy mists and fall rains have created roads with no bottoms. It will be very difficult to advance when orders to move are received.

Tuesday, November 14, 1944   Once again we are checking our guns and equipment. Have received extra ten-in-one rations for the drive. Extra boxes of .50-calibre and .30-calibre shells are stored by our guns. Also several cases of 57 mm antitank ammunition are placed where they can be found when needed. No one doubts now; we know the zero hour is near.

Wednesday, November 15, 1944   Finished most of our important and necessary duties yesterday. Nearly all are ready to roll as soon as we receive orders. We know the road ahead will be dangerous. We are realists, though. We know nothing happens unless someone causes it. We must move if this war is ever going to end. As night overtakes us, it seems to me that it will not be much longer until our forces move.

Thursday, November 16, 1944   Once again I stand and gaze into the blue sky as a roar is heard. Soon wave after wave of Flying Fortress and Liberator bombers pass over us. We see the long grey markers drifting down where they have passed. We hear the surging thunder of explosives ahead of our forces.

There is no doubt now; the long-expected drive is near. Tension mounts among the troops, as all know our few weeks of rest are nearing an end. Ahead on our mission lie death and destruction.

As darkness falls I'm trying to get some sleep, but for me it is not easy. The thoughts that keep running through my head. What lies ahead when the dawn breaks in the east? How many will fall on the drive? Many questions, but no answers can be found.

Friday, November 17, 1944   We move forward in the early morning hours to attack. The firing batteries of our artillery sound like thunder as they hammer targets close to the front line. Rockets cut flaming arcs across the dark sky, but as usual, battles are never won easy.

The enemy matches every shell we send over by returning two. As expected, we are finding this drive rough and very costly. The German defenses are much like the bloody hedgerows of Normandy.

Tanks spin and grip as sheets of water fly into the air. No dust to be found on this trip. Our forces are moving once more deeper into the homeland of Germany.

Our division encounters stiff opposition from our enemy. The route ahead is deep in mud, water, and debris. Beneath lie many mines, which soon take their deadly toll of men and machines.

Saturday, November 18, 1944   Morning comes, along with continuing assaults upon the heavily fortified enemy lines. Our forces are moving, but barely. Every yard gained is only by the supreme sacrifice of many of our troops. As we advance, many obstacles are being encountered. The precise fire of the 88 mm leaves many of our Sherman tanks burning, which sends columns of black smoke into the sky.

One unit of the medical aid station sets up a forward receiving station in the midst of the furious battle. By their total disregard of their own safety, many lives are saved.

Sunday, November 19, 1944   After a long, sleepless night of savage fighting, the dawn brings more of the same. Our forces are now receiving some new replacements. These troops are very young; most are in their teens. They have new clothes and clean battle gear. In a few days all of this will change. While talking to them, we learn some have been in the army only a short time. Many have less than one year of service. We try to reassure them that the field artillery is a good unit of our division in which to be assigned. But these young boys are very scared, as we were a few short months ago in Normandy.

As we are standing here by our roadblock talking, another scene tells all much plainer than words. A truck-load of replacement doughboys passes by on their trip to forward positions. Soon another truck returns full of troops. All are sleeping — forever!

Monday, November 20, 1944   Our division is still attacking the high ground. We find the enemy is dug in very well behind heavy fortifications. In spite of cold, unfavorable weather, we are advancing, but it is very costly.

The engineers are removing hundreds of mines along our route. Many of our tanks have been destroyed by these obstacles. Our P-47 Thunderbolts bomb a stubbornly held village in spite of cloudy weather. Although fires rage out of control and many buildings crumble, the end is the same as always. The doughboys have to move ahead to secure the ground.

Driving through the narrow streets of this little hamlet. Friend and foe lie where they have fallen. Smoldering ruins mark the site where homes once stood. Everywhere black smoke is drifting into the sky from burned-out vehicles along our route.

Once more some of us have been lucky and survived this last battle — many have not. Although we have witnessed this scene many times before, after each conflict the scar deepens.

Tuesday, November 21, 1944   Our attack against the stubborn German forces slows and finally comes to a halt. Of all the drives we've been on, this now has been the most muddy trip I can recall.

I'm trying to wash and shave, as we have some free time for a change. Doubt if I ever get clean again — some life. The mud is knee-deep on the level; I'll never complain of dust again. Our quarters for the night are very large, as we are outside in this weather.

Wednesday, November 22, 1944   Another day finds us still in this terrible place. Of all the destruction we have seen in Europe, this is by far the worst. Total devastation is the only way one can describe this region. Nothing can compare with this desolate and ruined area.

Our routes of advance have begun to resemble the terrible battlefields of World War I. This sector has been heavily shelled by American field guns, bombed, and now tank fire. Livestock lay stiff-legged in the fields. Over all this dreadful and appalling sight is the pungent odor of flame and death.

We are faced with a new menace. Every ten minutes the German robots pass over us. Although they seldom hit near the front, there is plenty of destruction from them in the cities of Belgium and England. Many cities that were untouched when we passed through are now being reduced to rubble.

Thursday, November 23, 1944   Morning finds all units busy once more with guns and equipment. Our maintenance battalion is placing sandbags on the front of the tanks for added protection from the dreaded 88s.

As our division pauses to regroup, we find another obstacle confronting us. The enemy has blown a dam on the Inde River. Now some of our task-force positions are flooded under nearly five feet of water.

Giant German searchlights have been installed by the foe near the front. Movement by our troops is seriously hampered by this latest development.

Friday, November 24, 1944   It is raining hard as our gunner informs his crew that we have lots of work to do on our track and guns. Most of the day is spent carrying out these orders. By nightfall our job is finished and we are soaked to the skin.

The evening hours bring the Jerries in the sky above our positions. A large number of antipersonnel bombs are dropped among our forces. We are fortunate that there are few casualties, but some equipment is destroyed.

Saturday, November 25, 1944   As the gray light comes in the east, our spearhead columns take to the roads again. Our crew is still attached to Headquarters, which is very close to the action.

Due to the deep mud on the roads, some of our tanks

become mired in the soft, sticky terrain. Now they are at
the mercy of the dreaded enemy antitank guns. Although
our maintenance works frantically to free them, many are
sitting ducks to the enemy fire. A large number of Sherman tanks can be seen burning in the sea of mud ahead of
us. Again we are paying a high price for our advance.

Sunday, November 26, 1944   Our 83rd Armored Reconnaissance Battalion has suffered heavy losses in this
drive. Their mission is to locate enemy positions. Several
of their armored cars were hit and left burning.

As the day drags by, our objectives are finally reached,
in spite of adverse weather conditions. Mounds of dough-
boy equipment testify to the high price we pay. Is it worth
it?

Monday, November 27, 1944   The village where we are
bivouacked is in ruins. We are getting used to finding this
on our latest trip. Shelter is going to be hard to find for so
many troops. There are no German civilians anywhere in
our sector. I can understand the reason. Who would want
to remain here?

We received orders to dig in for a short time. The Roer
River is just ahead of our division. Always one more river to
cross; must have been a hundred since our landing at
Omaha Beach.

Tuesday, November 28, 1944   A large number of Jerry
planes were over during the night. We observed flares and
bombs being dropped, but they did very little damage in
our area.

We learned the 1st and 104th Infantry are replacing
most of our sector. The line appears to be an artillery duel
supported by infantry. Our most-distant penetration is the
Roer River.

Wednesday, November 29, 1944   Today is my grand-
pa's birthday. Strange I would remember it in these sur-

roundings. I am looking ahead to eating birthday cake
with him next year. Received several letters from home at
mail call. Don't know when I will have time to answer
them.

Pulled guard on our gun for three hours during the
night. It was so dark I could see only a few feet ahead, but
had no trouble. However, I was ready to crawl in my bedroll
when relieved.

Thursday, November 30, 1944   Morning finds us
busy with maintenance. All guns and vehicles are covered
with a thick coating of mud. This must be removed and
our gun cleaned and oiled in order to be ready for our next
move. Sometimes it is a never-ending operation.

Our driver, Farr, is searching for some warm clothing
for his watchdog. Should have no problem in finding what
he needs. The wrecked homes have ample supplies of
everything, although some of the contents are not in the
best condition.

Friday, December 1, 1944   As I crawl out of my bedroll
this morning, it is very noticeable that the weather is
turning much colder. Winter will soon be upon us. No
matter how one looks at the future, it is bleak.

Our crew is living in a house again, or what remains of
one. At least our shelter is much warmer than out in the
open. Will have to look for some fuel for our stove. Have set
up our gun in front of our dwelling. The front is quiet now,
not much excitement, except air raids and robots.

We heard some weird tales about chimney details. It is
going to be necessary to have a man on every roof. What is
to be his duty? Every soldier must take his turn refueling
buzz bombs and bending chimneys to allow the robots to
pass on over the Stolberg-Breinig-Busbach area!

Saturday, December 2, 1944   Received a load of coal
with the compliments of the German Army. They were
going to use it but had to leave; too bad for them. This fuel
makes a hot fire.

Our crew would be in fine shape if a good cook could be found. We have plenty of cooking utensils, having located them in our recent travels.

Sunday, December 3, 1944　　Three years ago I came into the United States Army. How well I know the date. Where will I be one year from today? Looking ahead, the future is not very rosy. Although I am not in the best of surroundings, I am still in good health. Many of our buddies are not with us anymore.

Monday, December 4, 1944　　Another quiet day. The Germans fire an artillery barrage once in a while to inform us they are still in the vicinity. Very few Jerry planes have been seen the past few days. No one seems to be very busy in our area, as most of the necessary tasks have been taken care of the past few days.

Tuesday, December 5, 1944　　Managed to get up a poker game this evening. It is good recreation and there isn't much of anything else going on. All of our crew are still eating K rations. I'll sure be glad to see our kitchen truck when it shows up. In this cold weather a hot meal would taste good. The weather is still dreary and gradually becoming colder each night. The roads and fields are still very wet, which adds to our problems.

Wednesday, December 6, 1944　　We had a big poker game again this evening and as usual I ended up winning most of the money. There is no place to spend it and we can only mail a small amount home.

Seems to me we are all between the rock and the hard place and of course it does no good to complain.

Thursday, December 7, 1944　　Three years ago today this war started for us — a long distance from here. When will it end and the terrible suffering be over? This topic is the main conversation among our troops.

As evening comes I notice some of the water and mud

is drying up. Winter is very close and I'm not looking forward to it.

Friday, December 8, 1944   All of our crew started eating at the kitchen truck today. The hot meals sure do taste good and are very welcome.

Some would like to see our crew on KP duty, but no one wants our job on the antitank gun. So there is nothing they can do about that little detail.

All of our battery is at the front now. They rarely get this close to the action. Still our area is very quiet, which makes me feel uneasy.

Saturday, December 9, 1944   My mail is just now catching up with me. Sure is great to hear from home.

A large amount of work is being done on the roads by our engineers and the German civilians. After locating a rock quarry, the large holes are filled with heavy stones. Not much else can be done in the way of repairs, as it is still rainy.

Sunday, December 10, 1944   We learned today that our division is now in reserve, supporting the 1st and 104th Infantry. Near noon an enemy barrage hit a kitchen truck direct. Lost a couple of good cooks, who will be hard to replace. Our crew was ordered up closer to the front. We spent several hours doing some indirect firing in the direction of the enemy.

Monday, December 11, 1944   Morning finds more heavy rain coming down on our already soaked area. Maintenance is spending a good share of the time pulling vehicles out of holes where they have become mired. Our crew is taking advantage of our dry quarters in getting some much-needed rest. Except for guard duty, no one is very busy.

Tuesday, December 12, 1944   Dawn finds the rain still

coming down in this desolate sector of the Rhineland. The sticky clay clings to everything it touches. Most of our spare time is spent trying to keep our guns and equipment dry and ready.

Wednesday, December 13, 1944   Our crew spent the largest part of the day moving into another home. Finally managed to find a nicer place than the one we have been occupying. It used to be modern before the war. I'm sleeping on the couch, which is in good condition. This dwelling is by far the best accommodations we have found since leaving the hotel back at the edge of Germany. I'm sure these comforts cannot last, but they are appreciated while we are here to use them.

Thursday, December 14, 1944   We are still in our nice, dry house. Any shelter is good, as we are still having foul weather. This is indeed luxury that we are not accustomed to. Farr located a radio during his search of our house, and we are listening to some Kraut music. Can't understand the words, but the melody is relaxing. Found a washing machine in the basement, which we are putting to good use.

The line is stable most of the time. When things become quiet, I begin to feel uneasy, as something always happens.

Friday, December 15, 1944   I walked over to see Bowden and Irish at the ammunition train this morning. They finally received orders to move closer to the front. They were almost too late, as most of the livable shelter had been taken over by troops of other units.

Irish believes this sector will be our winter quarters. Would be fine by me, if I could stay in the house where we are living.

Saturday, December 16, 1944   Awoke this morning to remembering a strange dream I had last night. In this dream many German planes were bombing and strafing our forces. Also enemy paratroopers were being dropped behind our lines. A terrific battle was raging and many of our tanks were burning.

I related this strange dream to my gun crew. All have a good laugh at my expense. Sam then tells me I have been reading too many war stories. But this continues to bother me, as I've never had this happen before, as all my dreams were of home.

We are startled to find my dream is indeed becoming a reality. We learn these developments as reports begin coming into our division command. Dreams can come true! There is a great deal of activity in our sector.

Spearhead in the West

Spearhead in the West

Spearhead in the West

THROUGHOUT HIS SERVICE in the European theater, Willis was assigned to an M3 half-track (*top left and right*). The M3 was a workhorse of the Allied mechanized forces, being put to use as a prime mover for towed artillery, a cargo transporter, and an armored personnel carrier. Willis's position was on the .50-calibre machine gun in a ring mount next to the driver (*above*). The machine gun had been intended for antiaircraft defense, but because his half-track was subject to few attacks by German fighters or dive-bombers, he used it mainly for the kind of saturation fire against suspected snipers' positions that the American troops in Europe quickly adopted.

Spearhead in the West

THE MAINSTAY of the American mechanized forces like the 3rd Armored Division was the M4 Sherman tank (*above*). In spite of its high profile and relatively thin armor, the Sherman's power-traverse turret and its superior reliability and maneuverability made it effective against German armor in the kind of open terrain shown here. But when it lost these advantages in the deep mud the Allied forces encountered in the fall of 1944 and in the dense forests of the Ardennes in December, hundreds of Shermans were lost.

78

Spearhead in the West

Spearhead in the West

THE HEDGEROWS of Normandy at first proved a powerful ally of the German defenders, but American tank forces soon began to add plowlike teeth (*above, left*) or bulldozer blades (*above, right*) to the front of their Shermans. These allowed the tanks to smash through the hedges without exposing their lightly armored undersides to German antitank fire. The gaps these specialized tanks left also provided other vehicles and infantry with openings in the hedges that had not been zeroed in by German artillery (*below*). As Willis notes in his diary, the crossroads and other regular openings often had been, and they could become, killing zones for the advancing American columns.

St.-Lô

79

Spearhead in the West

Spearhead in the West

Spearhead in the West

ENEMIES that the 3rd Armored Division could not defeat so easily were the Germans' own armor and antitank weapons. The various models of the German 75 mm gun provided the main armament for many tanks, including the Mark IV, the German tank the Allies most often met in the early fighting (*top left*), and tank destroyers, like the *Jagdpanzer* IV (*top right*). It was also found on many assault guns, though the StuG III assault gun shown here (*above*) is armed with a 105 mm howitzer for use against infantry.

WILLIS, like most American troops, reserved his greatest respect for the German 88 mm gun. Whether employed as a towed gun, like the captured gun shown above, or as the main armament for the greatly feared Tiger and King Tiger tanks and a variety of self-propelled guns and tank destroyers, the 88 was more than a match for the American armor that opposed it. The Germans also employed the *Panzerfaust* (*right*), a rocket-powered antitank weapon that provided the inspiration for the American bazooka (and that Willis sometimes refers to as a bazooka). It is appropriate, in fact, that the accompanying photograph shows a *Panzerfaust* being wielded by an American soldier, because some American units used captured *Panzerfausts* whenever they could, as they were more effective against German armor than their own bazookas.

Spearhead in the West

81

DURING THE NORMANDY CAMPAIGN, Willis's gun crew was assigned to aid in the defense of the 3rd Armored Division's self-propelled artillery batteries. At first the division had only the M7 (*above*), which was simply a 105 mm howitzer mounted on an M3 tank chassis. Soon, however, it received the M12, which was armed with the heavier and longer-ranged 155 mm gun (*below, left and right*). These self-propelled guns allowed the divisional artillery to keep up with the rapidly advancing armor and mechanized infantry.

The XX Corps

FOR PROTECTION against local German counterattacks, the self-propelled gun batteries relied to some extent on the division's tank destroyers (*above*), in addition to the towed guns of the type manned by Willis's gun crew. The tank destroyers (TDs) were generally dispersed among the forward batteries, but not until late in the war, when they began to be rearmed with 90 mm guns, were they very effective against German armor. Though they resembled tanks, the American TDs were not heavily armored, and the TD crews who lived the longest were those who remembered that they could not simply stand and duel with a German tank under any conditions. As with the Sherman tank, the TD's superior mobility was its best defense.

AS WILLIS OFTEN NOTES in his diary, the rapid advance of the 3rd Armored Division often depended on its combat engineers' ability to build reliable temporary bridges to replace the permanent spans blown up by the retreating Germans as a delaying action. The bridges might be either the rapidly assembled Bailey bridges that spanned streams and the smaller rivers (*above*) or the floating pontoon bridges constructed across the larger rivers (*below*). The division used the pontoon bridge shown here to cross the Rhine for its final push deep into Germany.

84

6
Ardennes:
The Frozen Hell

As THE ALLIED ADVANCE had rolled rapidly through Belgium, one obstacle — the Ardennes — had split their forces like a boulder in a stream, with General Omar Bradley's 12th Army Group flowing south of the Ardennes toward the Saar and Montgomery's 21st Army Group flowing north of the forest toward Holland and the vital German industrial district of the Ruhr. To the Allied commanders, the rugged, heavily forested Ardennes seemed a virtually impenetrable barrier both to an Allied advance and a German counterattack. In retrospect, this conclusion is surprising, because Hitler had used the Ardennes as his gateway into France in the spring of 1940. Nevertheless, the result of the Allies' mind-set was that the Ardennes sector was only lightly held by Allied forces when Hitler again launched a major assault through the familiar forest roads and trails in December 1944.

Hitler's goal in this offensive was to push northwest out of the Ardennes across the Meuse at Liège and Namur and then on to Antwerp to cut off the Allied forces that had flowed north of the Ardennes. The intention was to create a second Dunkirk that would relieve the pressure on the western front and give him time to deal with the rapidly advancing Russians in the east. Since September he had been quietly amassing more than 200,000 troops and 1,500 armored vehicles and the accompanying materiel in Germany across the Our River from the Ardennes. He delayed the actual assault until he could be assured of at least six days of bad weather. This would ground the Allied fighter-bombers — which even Hitler had learned to fear. The German assault finally struck early in the morning of December 16, and it was this assault that sent the 3rd Armored Division dashing southwestward on the morning of December 17 in what seemed to the troops to be a bewildering retreat.

With reinforcements at a premium along the northern shoulder of the ever-growing salient in the American lines, the 3rd Armored Division was split up. Its various units were sent to

85

block the path of the most serious German breakthroughs. Willis's antitank gun crew ultimately became part of the defense of the important road center of Marche, from which a highway led northwest to cross the Meuse at Namur, one of the Germans' main objectives. The town's importance became clear in the pounding the Allied forces sustained there from the 116th Panzer Division over the next several days.

But, as elsewhere all along the Bulge, repeated German assaults here failed to break through to the Meuse, and by the end of December it was clear that the offensive had run out of gas — quite literally, in fact, since the Germans had great difficulty in moving their supplies of gasoline to the front and were unable to capture significant Allied supply dumps. As a result, several of the major assaults simply ground to a halt when their vehicles ran out of fuel.

A secondary reason for deploying the 3rd Armored Division in the vicinity of Marche and the towns of Hotton and Grand-menil to the northeast was to screen the assembly of the U.S. VII Corps on the Condroz plateau to their rear. When the Allied counterattack began on January 3, the 3rd Armored Division was one of the lead elements in the drive to link up with General Patton's Third Army pushing north from the Bulge's southern flank. After a bitter struggle — as much with the weather as with the German troops — the western section of the Bulge was cleared by mid-January and the 3rd Armored Division was sent into reserve.

Sunday, December 17, 1944   We are awakened before dawn to receive startling news. The 3rd Armored Spearhead Division has orders to move out. What is going on? Our forces are moving back into Belgium. Something terrible has happened, as we have never moved back before. As I glance around at my buddies, I find their faces are drawn and tense. A sharp contrast from a few days ago. Gone is the carefree banter of yesterday, replaced by fear and uncertainty. Concern is felt by all.

Very quickly the convoys of our division move out onto the roads. We observe very familiar surroundings as we continue on our journey. One thing keeps bothering me, and I am sure it must be on everyone else's mind: Our division is headed west, away from Germany.

As night descends, we are now confronted by another menace. The roar of many planes fills the night skies. Soon we realize the bombers above the convoy are not friendly but are the dreaded Luftwaffe.

Now, for the first time in months, our columns are exposed to air attack. We again hear the scream of German dive-bombers as they peel in formation down upon our convoy. The sky is ablaze with color from enemy tracer fire, which is directed upon us. This action from the sky, followed by large explosions resulting from many bombs, soon turns our convoy into a scene of total confusion. However, after a time, order is restored and we once more move ahead. Our forces have suffered heavy losses from this air attack.

Many robot bombs pass over us on their mission of destruction. All of the large cities along our supply line are being pounded by buzz bombs.

We find our task force is stopped at Eupen, Belgium. As light comes, we see the area is alive with activity as more troops and equipment arrive. Many civilians are on the streets. All seem happy to see us moving back into Belgium.

Monday, December 18, 1944   Dawn finds us helping to round up enemy paratroopers who have been dropped behind our lines. This action is proving to be very dangerous, as many of the German troops are wearing American uniforms. We have been alerted to use skill and tactics in solving this hazardous operation. We are being given passwords which are changed often. We must be on our guard at all times. It is very crucial, often the difference between life and death.

The German Army has penetrated a sector of the American line to the south of our position. This is a very dangerous development and is rapidly growing worse. Our division has been ordered to proceed south and west to meet the armored forces of the foe.

At nightfall we leave Eupen, and our armored columns once more take to the roads. Only the roar of motors from our tanks can be heard as we move forward in search of the rising tide of enemy armor.

Tuesday, December 19, 1944   Moved forward all night in blackout. Are the Germans already in Paris? Rumors by the hundreds — no one knows where the enemy is located. I'm sure that we will find them at the end of our search!

These roads are a nightmare to be on at night. The fact that we are in strange territory makes the trip much more difficult. Added to these problems, the weather is turning bitter cold. Heavy fog is limiting visibility in many places. All are wet, muddy, and weary with fatigue, but still we drive ahead. We've had no sleep since leaving Germany. Some snowflakes are drifting down as we continue on our way.

Wednesday, December 20, 1944   Nightfall finds our convoy bivouacked in a small Belgian village. An old couple insists that our crew share their small home. I am fortunate in getting my first night's rest for several days. I have no difficulty in getting to sleep, as my resting place is a large wooden bed complete with clean sheets and pillowcases. Has been a long time since I've had accommodations such as these.

Thursday, December 21, 1944   The next morning, after a good night's rest, we linger for awhile to thank our kind hosts. In talking to them, we discover they are very upset and scared of the Germans returning. With tears streaming down their weather-beaten faces, we are begged by our new friends not to leave them. Before leaving, we assure our patrons that more of our troops will soon be here. This information helped calm their fears. There was nothing more that we could do. We hear the sound of guns in the distance. It will not be very long until we reach our destination. We find the weather is turning colder. It is very difficult to keep warm, as our vehicles have no heaters.

As night descends, a heavy fog is settling around us. At times we must walk in front of our vehicles with a white cloth to lead the way. This is proving to be very dangerous for us. Some of our tanks have become lost due to low visibility. There is no time to search for them, as we must continue on our journey.

Friday, December 22, 1944   In the early hours our task force moves into the city of Marche. We receive orders that we must hold the road to Liège. There is not to be a retreat. The news is grim, as every available gun is being dug in for defense.

At last we are squarely in front of the powerful German juggernaut. The enemy forces, using a lot of armor, are attacking all along the battleline.

Some of our artillery batteries are firing direct, trying to stop the large German tanks. Clouds of smoke cover the terrain, and many of the villages are burning. The situation is fast becoming very desperate as our forces try to stop the onslaught.

Added to these adverse conditions, the weather is turning bitter cold. Fires can't be built because of enemy surveillance. The future looks bleak in the hills of Belgium.

Saturday, December 23, 1944   Since heavy German artillery shelling made sleep impossible, I was forced to roll out of my bedroll very early. Did not plan on eating any breakfast until I heard our kitchen truck was serving hotcakes. Our area received another heavy shelling while we were trying to eat.

Upon returning to the dwelling where we spent last night, we were again surprised. Only a shell of the house is standing, and it is still burning out of control. This house had received a direct hit. My luck is still holding, but some of my buddies were wounded.

Sunday, December 24, 1944   Last night I had another dream — someone close to me passed away. Hope all is well with my folks back home. It is impossible to write any letters now, as everything is in complete confusion.

Christmas Eve is a beautiful, clear, crispy cold night. Snow is falling slowly upon the pine forest, adding to the cover already on the ground. There is no spirit of Christmas among our troops as wave after wave of frenzied enemy soldiers attempt to overwhelm us.

Every available soldier is on the line this night with a weapon. Still, our defending strength is small. The Germans are trying assaults with large Tiger tanks. They loom awesome in the moonlight as their extremely accurate 88s rain death and destruction upon our armor.

Our heavy guns sound like thunder as exploding shells turn night into day. Supported by mortars, artillery, and rocket fire, the German line surges forward countless times.

Our line appears to be holding against overwhelming odds. Mounds of dead are left on the ground as the fresh white snow is turned red. Both sides are suffering heavy losses as the battle here in the Ardennes reaches an all-time peak of fury. A moment of crisis, and all hope the Krauts have lost.

Monday, December 25, 1944   I will never forget this Christmas Day here in the hills of Belgium. The presents being exchanged are much different from those found in the average home back in the States. I am sure that I'm correct in my knowledge of these happenings. Our division is receiving death and destruction from the Germans and we are trying to return the same greeting to them.

We find that one of our task forces is surrounded by enemy armor. Unable to break out and hopelessly outnumbered, these troops are at last ordered to destroy all their vehicles and other equipment. Many hours later, after infiltrating the German lines, the survivors, with blackened faces, stumble through the snowy hills to safety. The wounded and dead had to be left behind with volunteer medics. It was a sad night for us.

The enemy is continuing the attack all along the front. Many truckloads of frozen uniforms are observed on the roads after last night's battle. It is impossible to keep warm in this frigid weather, as we cannot build fires. The rolling fields are covered with snow, and every road is a sheet of ice. This adds to our problems as a cold wind blows across the Ardennes this gloomy Christmas Day.

Tuesday, December 26, 1944   As I crawl out from under our track this morning, there is one issue everyone is in agreement on. Winter is here to stay, even though no one is ready for the change in weather. It started to snow heavily again. Holes for shelter are impossible to dig, as the ground is frozen solid. Sure hope our crew can find warmer sleeping quarters than in a snowdrift.

Due to the hazardous operations of our engineers, miles of barbed wire and thousands of antitank mines are in front of our division. We are faced with a heavy blanket of fog that has settled in around the seemingly secure front.

Wednesday, December 27, 1944   As night fades into day, we receive new orders. We must hold our positions at all costs. We couldn't leave if we wanted to, as there is no place to go.

The battlefield has become an artillery duel as the tempo of fighting slows. This small village is in ruins. Very few civilians are still here, which comes as no surprise to us. Some of the buildings are made livable by boarding up shattered windows and installing field stoves. Since there are not enough army stoves, many civilian ones are found. Still, many of our troops are without heat of any kind.

We find that besides being thrust into a savage battle to stop the German drive, the weather has also become an obstacle to survive.

Thursday, December 28, 1944   Dawn breaks bright and clear. The rays of the bright sun reflect sharply against the white blanket of snow. Standing in nearly a foot of snow, I hear the roar of many planes as they echo through the pine trees in this valley. Seconds later the sky is filled with dive-bombers arriving to assist our forces. As usual, these planes are in groups of four. Some do not return to their bases. We see one crash and explode behind the enemy lines. Black smoke rises from the crash site as roaring flames are seen plainly from our position.

The attack by our P-47 Thunderbolts continues most of the day. This is the first clear day we have had to enable our friends in the sky to really assist our forces. Up to this time we have received very little close air support since arriving from Germany. The foul weather has kept the planes grounded most of the time. Heavy snow and ground fog have been with us since the breakthrough by the enemy.

Friday, December 29, 1944   Our lines of communication are now improved, due to the efforts of the 143rd Armored Signal Battalion. Working around the clock in sub-zero weather, this job has been one of the most hazardous of all. Icy roads and drifting snow have made this task a terrifying ordeal.

Our division is still locked in bitter battle with the German armor. Everywhere along the front we see the black smoke from burning tanks. Often when these war machines are hit there is no time for the crew to escape the raging fire which engulfs them. Then the tanks become coffins for the trapped troops. It is a very sobering task to remove the crew from their burned-out shells.

Even now our medics can be seen on the roads bringing out the wounded from the flaming holocaust. We learn that our line of defense is holding fast.

Saturday, December 30, 1944   Morning comes too soon for us. All is the same as the battle continues without let up. Soon we will know if we can contain the surge of the enemy. We have been told that the next few hours are critical.

Our division is now being supported by heavier artillery cannons. These guns are nearly as large as trees. They are 240 mm and require two half-tracks to move them. They are equivalent to the large German railroad guns. These large weapons of war are a welcome addition to our artillery batteries. Their firepower thunders as our forces try desperately to stop this attack.

Sunday, December 31, 1944   Today we learn that the enemy is giving up some of the ground they have held for days. This is the first good news our forces have received since our arrival here in these snow-covered hills nearly two weeks ago.

There are many reasons why the American army has been able to contain the savage onslaught. Clear weather helped save us, as our planes have been able to carry out their missions the past few days. Another reason is the supreme sacrifice of many of our troops. War is such a waste of life.

As the old year ends on the battlefield of the Ardennes, the fierce drive of the enemy has been stopped.

Monday, January 1, 1945   A new year is beginning. What does it hold for us?

An infantry division takes over the sector that we have been holding. Our division has new orders and is moving back for regrouping. There is to be a short breathing space as we take stock of the operation concluded and prepare for the offensive drive ahead. Now our forces must drive the Germans back to where the front was before the breakthrough.

Our victory has been too close for comfort in preventing the success of the German Army. The enemy advance has ceased in flame, death, and destruction. All of our units are low in manpower and equipment, as well as supplies.

Tuesday, January 2, 1945   We are located in the small villages of Ouffet and Ocquier in Belgium. We are getting replacements and new equipment. Everyone is busy, as a new battle looms ahead. The 703rd Tank Destroyer Battalion is back with us after having been loaned to another division.

The weather is still bitter cold as we go about our duties of getting the guns and ammunition ready. A strong wind is blowing out of the north across the snow-covered hills. This is another grim reminder of what lies ahead. Tanks and tracks are as cold as iceboxes as we prepare to move. Vehicles have no heaters because they would cause the crews to fall asleep.

Trench foot and frostbite become occupational diseases to our troops in this sub-zero weather. It is as if we are living in a white hell, and indeed that is the case.

Wednesday, January 3, 1945   The 3rd Armored Division moved out today in an opening attack against the Germans. Very soon the familiar villages and countryside we recently left come into view again. The ruined towns filled with charred, burned-out tanks are grim reminders of the past few weeks. We see splintered trees, snow packed with soot left by shell and mortar bursts.

In very difficult terrain, we are advancing against heavily fortified lines. Our attack in force is to meet the Third Army. This area is very hilly and heavily wooded. Evening brings a heavy snowstorm.

Thursday, January 4, 1945   Our crew was very lucky last night. We found a barn full of straw to sleep in. It was great to be able to get in out of the heavy snowstorm. This is the first time I have been warm since leaving Germany. Thought about remaining here but decided against that idea, so will have to move on.

We met a farmer who tried to give us some instructions. He was very excited and told us not to burn any of his posts to keep warm. We can't build a fire anyway, as the enemy lines are very close. Doubt very much if he could have prevented us from using his posts, had we decided to burn them. Most of the civilians are very cooperative. They are also very scared, which is sometimes the reason for their behavior.

Friday, January 5, 1945   Today our spearhead task forces are driving ahead in the bitter, crisp cold. There is an icy, paralyzing mist over the entire battlefront. A cloud of fine, driving snow leaves every tree silvered. The Ardennes looks like a Christmas card, but in that it is deceptive. It is agony all the way.

Even our Red Cross medics are hard-pressed to keep their blood plasma and other supplies from freezing. Syrettes are tucked into armpits so they can be used later to ease the pain of our wounded. Blood plasma, which saves so many lives, is carried under the hoods of medical peeps. The motor warmth keeps the distilled water from becoming ice.

Deep snowdrifts cover many fields of antitank mines. These winter conditions also make foxhole construction a nightmare. Over all of this man-made hell, the ceaseless wind blows, making visibility near zero at times.

Saturday, January 6, 1945   The weather is still very severe. Sub-zero temperatures have resulted in many troops having frostbite and frozen feet. Only the very critical soldier is evacuated from the front. Most are treated at the first-aid station and returned to duty. Our division is low on manpower.

I am fortunate in having received a pair of wool socks from home, so I have been able to keep my feet warm and dry. What we took for granted in the States is often critical here; many times it is the difference between life and death.

Although we are moving forward, our progress is very slow. Many obstacles have been placed in our path. In some places, trees have been dropped across our route of advance. Every delaying tactic is being used by the cunning foe. After being stopped to remove these barricades, we find all sites have been zeroed in for the German artillery fire.

As our troops move forward into the small town of Lierneux, we find this is the site of the Belgian institution for the mentally ill. The enemy booby-trapped all the buildings before leaving. Now our engineers are carefully removing the mines. This is a very tedious undertaking which takes several hours. Later, each building is deloused.

Sunday, January 7, 1945   Moving forward, another menace is being encountered by our troops. German forces, in their initial breakthrough of an infantry division, had captured a great deal of American equipment. We find enemy troops dressed in American uniforms driving captured Allied vehicles. Many have been able to infiltrate our lines. Most of the equipment has been painted white to blend in with the snow. Added to this latest threat, we find the enemy can speak English very well. Our troops have received orders to employ countermeasures to help solve this problem. We are again given passwords which change often. We must be ever alert.

We captured four enemy soldiers in a peep last night. They are going to be treated as enemy spies. It is not good to be found wearing an enemy uniform.

Monday, January 8, 1945   Our task forces are still advancing slowly. The attack against a stubborn enemy is proving to be very costly.

Everyone has the same idea of trying to find shelter as we stop for the night. It is quite a problem to be able to survive in the open during this freezing weather. It is surprising how nice some of these battle-scarred buildings look to us. At least they are shelter.

We have to battle the elements of nature as well as the enemy. There is nearly a foot of snow on the level. Some of the snowdrifts are several feet deep. It is beginning to snow again as night descends. The wind is rising again, and it looks as if a blizzard is on the way.

Tuesday, January 9, 1945   The scenery is beautiful but deadly and no time to enjoy it, as the roads are a slippery glare of ice. After six days of heavy combat, we have advanced only eleven kilometers.

We are encountering the large Tiger and Panther tanks. It has now become apparent that our Sherman tanks are no match for these fighting machines. When the outcome depends on armor or gun performance, they usually win. The German 88 mm is more powerful than our guns.

It is only by superior leadership, guts, and the spilling of blood that we are moving at all. The use of our artillery with concentrated fire is another factor in the destruction of the enemy armor.

Wednesday, January 10, 1945   Our planes are unable to assist us, as the weather is overcast. We are still driving ahead, but barely. An artillery duel brings heavy shelling all along the battlefront.

Trench foot, frozen toes, and battle fatigue are still with us. Replacements reach us, but we are still under-strength. They are very young and are confused and scared. No wonder, being thrust into a savage no-man's land, under the worst possible weather conditions. These young boys will know in a few days the horrible fatigue of the front-line soldier. Also, the dragging step and the glazed eyes that see only enemy. Some will come back, but many will never return. The clean, sharp boy with new clothes and chalked markings of P.O.E. on his helmet will be changed. In his place will be a man who at times does not look or act human at all. Like the rest of the spearhead soldiers, they will be dirty, frostbitten, and tired as they have never been before.

Thursday, January 11, 1945   As evening comes, our task-force columns drive forward in a continuing attack against a savage foe. In spite of cold, fear, and sudden death, we never falter.

There is too much blood on the snow by morning. Our route is lined with smashed and cluttered buildings, some of which are still burning. We see many dead men in the snowy ditches. It seems so very unreal; it looks as if mannequins had been scattered along the wayside. But this they are not! Here is stark testimony as to the savage battles in the frozen hell of the Ardennes.

Friday, January 12, 1945   Dawn finds our forces once more entering a small Belgian village with narrow streets that are shell-marked. But we soon find it very different. The inhabitants of Parfondruy have all been brutally murdered by Nazi SS troops. Everywhere in the streets, homes, and places of business the scene is the same. Most of the slain are old people, but some are mere children. This atrocity is senseless. Although we have seen death often in the past months, nothing can compare with this slaughter. All are upset by what it has been our misfortune to discover.

Saturday, January 13, 1945   I have been transferred temporarily to an ammunition track, as they are low in manpower. We are working around the clock hauling shells to the front to supply our firing batteries. Night driving on the slick roads in blackout is resulting in many wrecks.

The enemy has blown a bridge on our route to slow our progress. The engineers are called upon to build a structure over the river. In mud and snow it is built in complete darkness despite harassing fire by the Germans. Some of our engineers are forced to wade in icy, hip-deep water to accomplish their mission. Their job is one of the most dangerous of all.

Sunday, January 14, 1945   I'm back on the antitank gun with my crew. Don't know how long I will be here, though. Our forces are finding the large tanks of the enemy very difficult to cope with. Many of our Shermans are left burning when they meet these huge machines. A single Panther tank dug in on a hillside caught our tanks by surprise, destroyed several, and managed to escape. A very heavy snowstorm makes surveillance near zero at times. The house we are in has suffered many hits by shellfire. Looked good to us, though, as the snow is coming down very rapidly.

Monday, January 15, 1945   After moving forward a short distance, we were lucky to find a red barn in which to spend the night. It is really quite nice, and we are snug as a bug in a rug, as there is plenty of straw for bedding. To keep us company there are several cows and a couple of horses and a jackass. They accommodated us by moving over, leaving room for us to sleep. It is a puzzle how these animals have survived the battles.

Tuesday, January 16, 1945   Rumors are that the Germans are trying to pull out of the pocket they are in. Would be great if the weather would clear up so our dive-bombers could assist our troops.

Today, as I had some spare time, I took advantage of the lull to write a few letters home. A couple of the boys went on furlough. Very few can leave the front at this time. Fighting is easing up some — mostly artillery duels.

A number of enemy tanks have been destroyed by concentrated shelling from our firing batteries. It is a satisfying sight to observe German tanks burning instead of ours. Mopping up of enemy pockets continues, but it is beginning to look as if the 3rd Armored Division's involvement in the Ardennes is nearing an end.

Wednesday, January 17, 1945   Found a small home for our quarters tonight. Located a good stove and have plenty of firewood, so we are in good spirits. Everyone is exhausted. I will sleep for a week if ever the time comes when we can relax.

Sounds as if the fighting is moving away to the east. Infantry divisions are replacing most of the armor on the front. Still plenty of snow on the ground, but it does not seem as cold. The wind has ceased blowing.

Thursday, January 18, 1945   The 3rd Armored Division is pulling back for regrouping. Must have replacements and new equipment before returning to Germany. Roads are lined with burned-out tanks and other weapons of war. This is all that remains of the bitter fighting of the past few weeks.

We see many Belgian civilians as the war moves away from here on to the east. They are returning to their homes, or whatever is left after the battles. Even though some have lost everything, they seem relieved for the first time in weeks. In their faces can be seen joy as these people happily hurry to their homes and villages. Many are walking, but some push carts, and a few are fortunate to have a horse or cow to pull their wagon.

Friday, January 19, 1945   Our convoy moved all night on strange roads in blackout. The route is covered with ice and snow, which is very slick and dangerous for travel. There is no sleep for anyone this night, as our trip is very nervewracking. One of the tanks missed a turn and fell over a high cliff. All are happy to see the light of day.

Saturday, January 20, 1945   It is beginning to look as if all will get some rest, and everyone needs sleep. Our force is bivouacked in another small village. Our crew is sleeping in a very nice home. The war has missed this place, as there are no battle scars.

I'm getting some water heated for a bath and then will try trimming my beard. I'm sure both are needed, as it has been a long time since I've had any time for this chore. We have started getting our meals at the kitchen truck once again. Sure is good to eat hot meals during this cold weather.

Sunday, January 21, 1945   Again our division is moving farther from the front. Stopping later, we are issued many new tanks. Other equipment is also being moved into our sector.

The snow is slowly disappearing, and green grass can be seen in many places. Some passes are available now, and I went on a convoy to Huy this evening. Didn't enjoy the trip, as it is hard to relax on such short notice.

Monday, January 22, 1945   Some of my buddies bought some cognac; the price was twenty dollars a bottle. That is too much money for me to spend. All of us are taking it easy and trying to relax as much as possible.

As I glance around, many familiar faces are missing. Young replacements are here in record numbers. Our division has suffered many casualties on the Ardennes battlefield.

Tuesday, January 23, 1945   We have been issued new clothes at the showers. I sure needed a change, as mine are very dirty and in tatters. It is also a nice experience to be able to take a bath without using my steel helmet for a basin.

A very few robot bombs are passing over our area. Hardly any Luftwaffe planes are to be seen in the sky.

It is beginning to look like an early spring, as the weather is turning lots warmer. The snow cover is rapidly disappearing, which is a very welcome sight.

Our battery is located in a pretty Belgian village. The people are very friendly. Sure would be great to remain here until the end of the war.

Wednesday, January 24, 1945   Our gun crew is still living in the same house. Wrote a long airmail letter home to Mom. I have almost caught up on my correspondence. I send V-mail most of the time. We have been receiving some recreation in the way of movies in the evening.

Everyone is busy during the day, as we have been informed there is a lot of hard work ahead in getting ready for Germany again. The new tanks being issued have larger guns and thicker armor.

Thursday, January 25, 1945   Received new orders that I am transferred to the ammunition train permanently. I'm now in the same track as my friend Bowden. Our driver, Glover, is from Oklahoma. Irish is also in this train.

Father has also been transferred and is now in a forward observer tank. This is a very dangerous job, but he asked for the position.

Friday, January 26, 1945   Although we are in a quiet place, another situation is with us again. This is boredom, which always happens after a period of time when our division is in reserve. Some of the evenings are spent playing poker. This recreation gives us something to do during our idle time. No one is very busy as the 3rd Armored Division gears up for the coming battles. All the snow is gone now, as the weather continues to turn warmer.

Saturday, January 27, 1945   Received some new orders early today as I am rudely awakened to find I am back on KP. My last KP detail was when our division was in England. I really am enjoying this duty, as there is plenty of good, warm food here. It sure is better than our own cooking of ten-in-one rations.

I learned that our ammunition train will have only K rations while on missions after ammunition.

Sunday, January 28, 1945   I have been busy most of the day cleaning and oiling my .50-calibre machine gun. Would rather have the one I had been using, but have no choice. My personal weapon is a Browning submachine gun. I still have the P-38 taken from the German captain we captured in Liège, Belgium. It is in my shoulder holster, but doubt if I even use it.

Monday, January 29, 1945   Some of the troops went hunting and bagged a few rabbits. We are having a big feast at our evening meal. Will be a welcome change from our regular rations, which are mostly in powdered form. Most of the time there is plenty of food. However, some meals have been postponed until a later date. I've yet to meet anyone who has gained weight since we came off the beaches of Normandy.

After searching several days, our crew finally located some cognac for the return trip to Germany. We miss Father, who is not here to provide beverages for us.

Tuesday, January 30, 1945   It is beginning to look as if we may be moving back into Germany real soon. I would like to remain here, it is so peaceful. I'm getting attached to the quiet way of life.

As I recall the events of the past weeks in the Ardennes, it seems like a bad nightmare. Will no doubt always remember the biting cold, snow, and ice, of never really being warm in the freezing weather. Also, the long march without sleep, of having to always be on guard against German paratroopers and agents dressed in American uniforms.

But even then there were good times to remember, as on December 24 and 25, when fleets of our heavy bombers filled the clear sky.

I remember standing in deep snow gazing up into the atmosphere as our planes seemed like tiny pieces of silver above the battlefield. When our hour of peril was the greatest and the outcome hung in the balance, their bombs of destruction helped to turn the tide of battle in our favor.

7

Back to Germany

WITH WILLIS'S PERMANENT TRANSFER to the 3rd Armored Division's ammunition train, he was taken out of the front lines. Thus, when his division was transferred back to their old pre-Bulge position near Aachen, Willis led the fairly quiet life of the support troops. In any case, the 3rd Armored Division was placed in reserve until it returned to combat in the crossing of the Erft Canal east of Düren in late February and in the occupation of Cologne in early March. Willis did, however, feel the effects of the German artillery and air bombardment designed to disrupt, and thus delay, the American operations. Though the German infantry and armor continued to resist every Allied advance, their ability to do so was much less than it had been as late as the previous November. In late March the 3rd Armored Division crossed the Rhine at Honnef, south of Bonn, and assembled in the bridgehead created by the 9th Armored Division's capture of the Ludendorff bridge at Remagen on March 7. By March 24, after another major buildup of Allied forces and materiel, the 3rd Armored Division was poised to push still deeper into Germany.

Wednesday, January 31, 1945   Morning finds the 3rd Armored Division on the roads heading back to Germany. After a couple of hours our track breaks down. Very soon we are alone in strange surroundings. At last the repairs are made and we move ahead. We have no idea where our convoy is now, so are heading due east. After becoming lost several times, our crew finally manages to catch up with part of our unit. On our return trip we find the snow and ice are gone. The route we travel is once again a sea of mud.

Entering familiar terrain, remnants of the Siegfried Line come into view. The shattered towns of Stolberg and Breinig bring back bitter memories of savage tank battles which raged here last September. We find the war has moved to the east. A great deal of activity is observed as the German people start to rebuild their towns.

Thursday, February 1, 1945   Morning finds our convoy halted in a small village near Aachen. After spending several hours in locating lodging for the night, we receive orders to move on. We are not too happy over this decision, as we had found a nice home.

Night finds our forces continuing to move along the roads. I tried getting some sleep in our track, but had no success.

Friday, February 2, 1945   Near dawn finds us bivouacked in another small town. Our crew was lucky to find a house with half a roof. Hope there is room for all of us on the dry side. All buildings are in a shattered state. The past few months of shelling have taken their toll.

This area is covered with land mines and booby traps. Many of our engineers are at their dangerous task of removing the explosives.

Saturday, February 3, 1945   While eating breakfast I noticed our kitchen truck parked only a few feet from a Kraut's grave. I doubt if this will spoil anyone's appetite, though. Nothing seems to bother us anymore after all we've seen.

Sunday, February 4, 1945   The 3rd Armored Division is in reserve again. It is mostly infantry holding the line at this time.

The enemy has had plenty of time to fortify his positions the past two months. It will be very difficult to penetrate through his defenses when we move forward once more.

It is still very overcast. Have received a lot of rain and ground fog most of the time.

Some of us attended a movie in a building near here this evening. It was about a war, which is not popular here.

As we left, the sky was ablaze as the Luftwaffe put on their show for us.

Monday, February 5, 1945   Near midnight a lone Jerry plane strafed the road in front of our living quarters. We were lucky, as no damage was inflicted.

Melting snow and heavy rains have swollen the Roer River. To further add to our many problems, the enemy has opened the floodgates. This maneuver resulted in a great deal of flooding. Orders for crossing the river have been cancelled until the water level lowers.

Tuesday, February 6, 1945   Some of the troops have received a new assignment. We are now engineers working on the roads. They are in terrible condition. The trucks are busy hauling rock from pits nearby.

The only equipment I have is a shovel which does not fit my hand. There is plenty of manpower, but not very much is being accomplished. May be forced to contract this operation if it is ever to be completed.

Wednesday, February 7, 1945   Another day finds me still working on the roads. Figured I was doing a good job of goldbricking yesterday, but I have a sore back. May have leaned on my shovel too often.

The roads are improving, so someone must be working. This is a very difficult job, as all routes are deep in mud and water. The rains have been with us since our return to Germany.

Thursday, February 8, 1945   Today more new equipment is being moved into our sector. The tanks are much heavier, with larger guns.

I'm still on the road gang; isn't too bad, as no one is working very hard. Much safer than up on the front. There seem to be more chiefs than Indians on this detail.

The ammunition train is much quieter than when I was on an antitank gun. It should be safer, but who can tell? Around here anything can happen and usually does. Hauling supplies through isolated enemy pockets is also very hazardous. The safest place would be a long distance from Europe.

Friday, February 9, 1945   Our engineers are still clearing roads and fields of mines. In some places they are very close together. The task of removing and destroying them is very dangerous.

Farr still has his dog with him. While we were down in the Ardennes he made a warm coat for Fritz to wear. He is still planning on taking him back to the States.

Saturday, February 10, 1945   One of the replacements, who had been with us just a short time, picked up an enemy gun which was booby-trapped. It was a very short war for him. Some of the boys had been telling him how fortunate he was to be in the field artillery. We never know from one minute to the next; the future is very uncertain.

No one has been very busy the past few days. All are wondering when the next drive will take place. I'm sure that information will come soon enough.

Most of the homes here are filled with furniture and personal belongings — nothing of value, however, due to the severe shelling of the past weeks.

Sunday, February 11, 1945   Some of the new troops are receiving combat training nearby. Consists mostly of house-to-house combat attack. A mock-up of a village has been set up for training.

Monday, February 12, 1945   I received a number of letters from home. As I'm not too busy, have been answering most of my mail. Now the days are beginning to drag, as we wait for new orders for the next drive.

Tuesday, February 13, 1945   We had some extra excitement in our area today. Some of us found a Kraut machine gun and did some firing into a high bank. In a couple of minutes a number of officers appeared. They must have thought a war was going on. Their reaction was not favorable to our target practice. We were informed to use only our guns when firing and to have them aimed toward the enemy. I'm sure all of us got the message. As for me, I'll use only my weapons now. The German guns have a different sound, which is very distinguishable.

Wednesday, February 14, 1945   Our crew spent most of the morning looking for nicer sleeping quarters. We had no luck, as most buildings are in terrible condition, so have decided to keep the bungalow we have been sleeping in. At least we have a roof.

Spent most of the evening playing poker. I was lucky to end up with most of the money.

Thursday, February 15, 1945   More letters from back home at mail call. All are well, which is good news. Answered with a couple of V-mail letters.

Heavy rain with fog is with us once more. This condition will make the muddy roads even worse for us to move on. Hope the weather improves soon. I venture out only when forced to.

Friday, February 16, 1945   Climbed out of my bedroll to find the sun shining with a clear day ahead for us.

The sound of planes fills the air, and several P-47 Thunderbolts come into view. They are busy most of the day strafing and bombing the enemy lines.

Later, one lone German jet aircraft was seen dropping two bombs near a bridge. The plane was moving so fast our antiaircraft crew could not get their guns in position.

Saturday, February 17, 1945   Although the weather is still cold, the sun shines brightly. The skies are filled with our dive-bombers resuming their attack on the city of

Düren. From our position fires can be seen burning. Mud and water still covers the roads, as the weather hasn't helped to dry them.

Sunday, February 18, 1945   Received a letter from home which informed me my friend Howard was killed on December 24 when his plane was shot down over Germany. I recall the dream I had on that date. I feel very much alone today!

Still not much doing except guard duty and routine checking of vehicles and guns. We must always keep all guns clean, oiled, and ready. Many times we have had only a moment's notice to defend ourselves. I've had so many close encounters with the enemy that I have learned to always be ready for anything.

Night brings a cold wind blowing out of the north. Still, it is warmer than last winter down in the Ardennes.

Monday, February 19, 1945   No one is very busy today. All are getting bored just sitting around waiting. We have been arguing most of the morning, and as usual the conversation ended with talk about women.

We received orders to work on the roads again. Added to this bit of news, the rain is coming down once more. So what else is new around here?

Tuesday, February 20, 1945   Today brings continuing activity around our sector. Many more tanks and guns are being located in the fields.

None of the ammunition trains have been on the roads for several days. The fields are stocked with ammunition for all of the guns. From past experience, I am sure we are getting close for more action against the enemy. We will not be here much longer.

Wednesday, February 21, 1945   Received a letter from a friend from back home. Stanley Crook was also down in the "Battle of the Bulge." His letter sounded as if he isn't too happy over being in Germany. He is one of many to express those views.

Near evening we received orders to be ready to move at a moment's notice. Once more the tension mounts as the zero hour draws near.

Thursday, February 22, 1945   The early morning hours echo with the roar of artillery fire from countless guns. Since sleep is now impossible, I tumble out of my bedroll and slip on my boots. At times even my footwear is not off my feet for days.

The weather has improved, and we hope our forces have air support when the drive comes. All assistance that is available will be needed. Everything is ready as we marshal our forces to penetrate the heavily fortified German line. We have not seen this much armor for a long time. The troops are in a better mood and seem more confident than when we first arrived back in Germany. The weather is warmer, too, which is a contributing factor.

Friday, February 23, 1945   In the misty morning hours the doughboys of the assault teams of the 104th Timberwolves move out in force. Many boats are lost on the swollen Roer River. German artillery and mortar fire is deadly against the attacking infantry. However, by the end of the day several bridgeheads are established on the east side of the river.

This action is very costly, as many men are drowned in the swiftly moving stream. During this operation these troops are under heavy machine-gun fire, which takes a deadly toll.

As night comes, the 3rd Armored Division has been placed on alert to move at a moment's notice.

Saturday, February 24, 1945   Another day finds our division still waiting. We are ready for the next move. Our 23rd Engineers have been busy building pontoon bridges across the Roer River. This news informs us that the fateful hour is near. Reconnaissance reports indicate the Germans have pulled much of their armor back to secondary defenses. The 8th and 104th Infantry Divisions are holding the bridgehead to the east of the Roer River. They have fanned out to establish a line for our forces.

Sunday, February 25, 1945   The Sabbath Day breaks cold with drizzling rain. Most of the secondary roads are impassable due to the thaw and heavy rains.

It is with these terrible conditions that the 3rd Armored Division receives march orders. In the misty half-light of dawn, the roar of motors from hundreds of tanks signals the attack and echoes through this valley. We are once more on our way deeper into Germany. Some of us will survive, while others will die — our fate is not in our hands. At least we are moving, and this our forces must do for this war ever to end.

After crossing the river we divide into separate task forces. As our columns drive forward, the rubble heaps of what were once towns come into view. The desolation and destruction staggers the imagination.

Our column pauses for a short time in the city of Düren. The statue of Bismarck is standing in a park, but nearly everything else has been leveled in this large town.

On the east side of the Roer River, the heat and fury seem to intensify as we drive forward. The shattered villages are very stubbornly defended by the enemy as we advance. Shells pass over us, and the constant chatter of machine guns can be heard everywhere.

Once again the pounding, smashing battle leaves buildings burning and vehicles overturned. Everywhere by the roadside are the dead and dying. The enemy rear guard antitank guns are very accurate, so many of our comrades are falling in the heat of the battle.

Monday, February 26, 1945   A heavy enemy artillery barrage sends our crew to the shelter of Mother Earth. How many times in the past months have I kissed the ground I walked on? If counted, the number would be considerable. We find that there is no shortage of ammunition from the German sector.

Near evening, I saw another enemy jet attempt to destroy a bridge. Again the target was missed, but the plane managed to escape our antiaircraft fire.

Tuesday, February 27, 1945   As our division moves ahead, more land mines are encountered, but there are fewer than when we first crossed the Roer River. The cunning Germans are using every means to delay or halt our assault. In some places trees have been dropped across our route. Another delaying tactic is a small robot tank fastened to a wire, which when tripped crosses the road in our path. Although loaded with explosives, this device has done very little damage.

We are lucky to have a battery of 155 mm artillery cannons attached to our division. They are dropping shells into the city of Cologne on the Rhine River.

Wednesday, February 28, 1945   Morning finds us crossing the Erft Canal, which is the last barrier before Cologne. Some of our tanks are on the broad plain before the Rhine River. Many of these towns have wooden barricades in the streets, but they do not slow our attack, as our firepower is awesome.

Our forces are in much the same position as the Germans were when they broke through our lines last winter in the Ardennes. This is not to imply that the war is nearly over. Many fights and hardships are still ahead for us. We do, however, continue to move forward, which is cause for all to feel more confident.

Our columns finally halt for the night in a small German village. Before we have time to camouflage our vehicle, a lone enemy plane flies low over our area. We hope this surveillance does not result in more German air action.

Our bridgehead forces are receiving heavy mortar

attack from the enemy, which is attempting to push us back across the canal. The thundering artillery batteries try to silence the German guns.

As dusk turns day into night, we find another threat descending upon us. Scores of Luftwaffe planes fill the sky over the battlefield. All night long their planes bomb and strafe our lines. There is a constant hum of aircraft, followed by the eerie whistle of the bombs. Loud explosions and flames rise into the sky. Tracers from antiaircraft guns light up the sky. We see several enemy bombers crash in flames, but still their attack continues as the long night drags on.

Soon the house I'm in is crowded with more of our troops from other homes, which have suffered hits. Irish is among the survivors seeking shelter with us. He is very lucky, having only bruises. The attack ceases near morning. Last night was the longest I have ever experienced.

Thursday, March 1, 1945   With the coming of dawn, we are able to see much more clearly the destruction caused by enemy aircraft. The peaceful village we entered yesterday is now a scene of total devastation. Everywhere we see wrecked homes, some of which are still burning from the raging fires created by the bombs. Many tanks and guns are also among the hits scored by the Germans. Black smoke rises from burned-out equipment.

The houses here are connected together, as in many cities of Europe. Now I am able to see plainly how close I was to death. Both houses connected to the one I was sleeping in were destroyed by the bombs. The house Irish was in had one side blown out. One of our buddies was coming through the door when the bomb exploded — he never had a chance. The other home suffered a direct hit by a bomb with a delayed fuse that went into the basement before exploding. Many troops were buried under the debris. Some of us spent the rest of the night digging them free. Our division had many casualties in last night's air raid. The enemy bombing was a terrible ordeal. Now many of our buddies will never see home.

Sabo, a close friend I had spoken to a few days ago, was sure the war would soon be over and just hoped he could hang on until that time. He will not be with us when we lay down our guns.

Another buddy, Abramowitz, is also among the dead. He was married and had two little boys back home. Saved most of his money and had told us of his plans for his family when he returned home.

Friday, March 2, 1945   We heard today that not one German civilian was injured. The town was crowded with them. No one could understand the reason for this, but later in the day we found all had deep air-raid shelters for their safety.

We want to leave this place as soon as possible. Too many close friends are dead after the German air raid, and many more are wounded. Most of them had been with us since Camp Polk. To have come so far and then this — so many gone.

The German raid was over all of the front. Hundreds of enemy planes were involved, and many were shot down by our ack-ack. Our forces suffered heavy losses. Last night will always be remembered by all who survived.

Saturday, March 3, 1945   I'm a very lucky soldier; my name was drawn for a pass to Paris. Only two can go out of our battery, and Sgt. Laszchuck and I had the good fortune to be the ones. Will be great to be away from the front for a few days. We are to leave most of our gear, as we will return. All we are taking are extra clothes and personal items. Irish loaned me some extra money, so I'll have plenty of cash.

Sunday, March 4, 1945   Our convoy left early in the morning loaded with happy troops. All are glad to get away from the battlefield. After several hours on the road, we finally arrive at Verviers, Belgium. Following a short delay, we climb upon the soft cushions of a small passenger train. It is sure a nice ride. The compartments on this train are much smaller than the ones in the States.

Seems strange back here, as if there wasn't a war. The people are very happy now that the Germans have left.

Monday, March 5, 1945   Our train reached Paris early in the morning. Everyone is in good spirits as we descend from the train to start our leave. Paris is very bright and gay compared to where we have been these past months. It is very much like the cities back home. From all appearances, the destruction of war has not touched here. The French are very friendly to us, and most are busy going about their jobs.

I'm trying to have a good time, but it is very difficult. It is hard to relax on such short notice. Will be rough to return to the front in Germany.

Tuesday, March 6, 1945   I'm convinced this is the life for me. I never roused out of bed until near noon, then ate a hearty meal. Walked around Paris in the afternoon and found it much larger than I had imagined. I saw the Arc of Triumph and several large cathedrals.

In the evening, I took in the Follies. It was a very good show, with many pretty girls taking part. Such a change of pace the past few days, it is hard to adjust. However, a different atmosphere is real nice.

Wednesday, March 7, 1945   I arose early and after eating went shopping at several large stores. Everything is very costly. Ended up spending about three months' pay buying gifts for my family back in Iowa. Had all presents mailed home from the store where I purchased them. Saved me some extra time, which I don't have much of while here in Paris.

Spent the rest of my leave sight-seeing. Paris is a very beautiful city. I would like to return here someday. Would like to take some pictures, but I'm low on cash now. Really doesn't matter, as I will have no use for money back in Germany.

Thursday, March 8, 1945   Another day finds me back on the train headed east toward the front. No one wants to return to the battlefield, but we have no choice in the matter. I am one tired soldier. Must have taken in too many sights in my short stay. Spent all of the money but had a good time, so I have no regrets.

Sgt. Laszchuck and I got separated on the first day and I never saw him again until we met at the train for the return trip.

We are having a swell time riding on this little train. The only civilians are the crew, who don't bother us. Seems to be plenty of drinks among the troops, as no one goes thirsty.

Friday, March 9, 1945   We are still riding the quaint little French train. The countryside and towns we pass through are very picturesque. Nothing along our route is disturbed, unlike the area we came through from Normandy.

The homes observed along our journey are very neat with their straw-covered roofs. Someday, after the war is over, I would like to return for a visit here and also the other countries I've been in. Hope by then the scars of war will be gone.

I saw many more beautiful cathedrals, which are in very good condition.

Saturday, March 10, 1945   Our train arrives in Verviers, Belgium, near noon. We leave the soft cushions for the hard wooden seats of army trucks. It doesn't take very long for me to realize my leave is nearly over. By late afternoon we once more see the familiar Siegfried Line of Germany.

Night overtakes us, and very soon the bright flash of the large guns is seen to the east of our convoy. The rest of our journey is made in blackout. My eyes should be like a cat's from peering into the darkness.

Our convoy arrives in Cologne at last. At the edge of the city we learn our troops have captured the first major city of Germany while we were on leave.

Everywhere I look there is ruin and desolation. The enemy troops that had time have fled to the east side of the Rhine. Cologne is a dead town. Although the city is quiet now, we learn that the scene was very different a few days ago. Then the wide streets and buildings were places of action in which furious battles raged as our troops fought their way into the city. Tank battles were everywhere, and black smoke covered the entire city like a dirty blanket. After hours of heavy artillery fire, our infantry moved ahead through the alleys and streets. The sound of machine guns and small-arms fire could be heard plainly as friend and foe fell in the bloody conflict. As usual, many buildings were burning.

Among the ruins and rubble was a sniper's paradise, and each had to be found and smoked out. A sniper's fire is deadly, as each one is an expert marksman.

Our forces suffered heavy losses. War is never one-sided, no matter what historians write. They record battles but often miss the heart of the issue.

Glancing around the familiar faces, I note some are missing. No need to ask questions; I know the reason. Maybe someone volunteers information, maybe not. Makes no difference. We shrug our shoulders and go on our way. To a civilian, this attitude might seem indifferent or not caring. This couldn't be farther from the truth. We all care, but there is nothing we can do about it. And the position we are in now, we cannot afford to let our emotions get the best of us. No one wants to be thousands of miles from home fighting a savage war, but here we are. All any of us want is for this war to end so we can go home. Many will never return to their families.

One of the spearheads liberated the inmates of Staatsgefaengnis Prison. Eighty-five of the original eight hundred inmates are still alive but in very poor health. All suffer from malnutrition and many have typhus.

Sunday, March 11, 1945   Morning finds our ammunition train moving to the east and south. Late afternoon finds us pausing at a large farmhouse. All of the buildings are in a square with a huge courtyard in the center, and there are many kinds of livestock on this farm. Some of the homes have civilians living in them. None are friendly, which is fine, as we are not on a goodwill tour. We are told by these farmers that all of the slave labor has left. Now the Germans must do all of their own work.

We located a good, deep air-raid shelter in the cellar of the home in which we are now living.

Monday, March 12, 1945   Irish is helping to outfit me with a new bedroll. I sure needed one, as mine was in rags. I'm spending this evening catching up on my correspondence. This is the first time I've had to write letters home for weeks.

Once again we hear many rumors. This always happens when we have a few days' rest. Some don't believe we will cross the Rhine River. I'm confident the 3rd Armored Division will be out in front on the next drive.

Everyone is eating at the kitchen truck once more. It is much tastier food than we used to cook when I was on the antitank gun.

Tuesday, March 13, 1945   Received news that the 9th Armored Division has seized a bridge intact across the Rhine River at Remagen. Also that the Germans are using every means of trying to destroy the crossing.

Morning finds us on the road heading south, where the bridgehead is forged. After several hours our forces enter a small mining town, where we bivouac. Like many enemy villages, it shows the scars of the war. Later we are lucky to find shelter in one of the homes.

Wednesday, March 14, 1945   This morning I'm on a short walk to survey my area. It is very quiet — a sharp contrast from a few days ago. This would be an ideal place to remain until the war is over, but this will never happen.

Received orders to clean and oil all our guns. Also tanks, tracks, and other vehicles are being readied for our next move.

Glover found a radio here in the basement, so we are listening to some music. Our buddies have joined us for this new entertainment.

Thursday, March 15, 1945   Bowden and I took a tour of the town. While on our trip we saw some mines and factories with very modern machinery. There are many German civilians in this town. They are busy at their jobs and are not causing any trouble.

The 3rd Armored Division is still on the defense status. How much longer this will be we do not know. All are taking advantage of this lull by getting some much-needed rest.

Friday, March 16, 1945   A few Jerry planes are seen flying over at night. It is very easy to distinguish their aircraft from ours. The engines of the enemy planes sound as if some spark plugs are missing.

The German cities are being pounded by our large air fleets. Allied heavy bombers fly at every hour of the day and night on their deadly missions. As our ground forces move forward, targets for our planes are much more difficult to locate.

Saturday, March 17, 1945   I have been busy most of the day getting all of my equipment in good working order. Spent several hours washing my clothes. Hope the sun continues to shine so they will dry. I'm now ready for an evening of entertainment, which will be difficult to find.

Sunday, March 18, 1945   We had orders to clean and service our track today. With all of our crew helping, we were done by noon. Then Bowden and I oiled and checked all of our machine guns again. I have several extra barrels for my .50-calibre. It is quite a task keeping my sub-

machine gun free from rust in this rainy weather. It has
never jammed, though.

Monday, March 19, 1945   All of the towns and fields
are filling with troops and war weapons. Many heavier new
M26 Pershing tanks are visible.

Nearly all who were not on guard attended the movie
this evening. Our battalion found a dance hall to use for
our movie theater. The projector broke down a dozen
times, so everyone lost interest before the show ended.

Tuesday, March 20, 1945   Many rumors are heard
throughout our unit. Still the talk is that we won't cross
the Rhine River. I'm not listening, as I'm sure we will be
there when the drive comes.

Some of the new Pershing tanks are being brought
into our division. They are larger than the Shermans and
have heavier guns. All the troops are ready, as our forces
are brought up to full strength.

Wednesday, March 21, 1945   After breakfast, we receive orders to move. In a short time our convoy is on the
roads moving south again. All seem in good spirits as we
get under way. Morale has always been good in our
division.

After a long, dusty ride, we reach the Rhine River. At
the town of Honnef our engineers build pontoon bridges to
use for crossing the river.

Thursday, March 22, 1945   I was lucky at mail call
today. Received nearly a dozen letters from home. Some are
over a month old, but at least they are catching up with
me. I'm trying to answer some, as I'll be busy in a few days.

Irish and I spent the evening talking. He informed me
that this would be our last drive. I replied that I hoped we
were both around when it ends.

Friday, March 23, 1945   Our ammunition train is very

busy. Unloaded all tracks and crossed the Rhine River for a new supply of ammunition.

Everyone is tense as we make final preparations for the next fateful attack. As usual, many new faces are seen among the troops. Some of the new replacements have never been under enemy fire. They will not have much longer to wait until they will know firsthand.

Saturday, March 24, 1945   This morning we received orders through combat command channels. The 3rd Armored Division is moving out at dawn in full-scale attack.

The night hours echo with the thunder of artillery fire from hundreds of guns as the initial assault gets under way. Night becomes as day amid the exploding shells. The 1st Big Red One and 104th Timberwolves Infantry Divisions move slowly ahead trying to widen the bridgehead.

All of us in the Spearhead Division try to get some sleep, but rest does not come easy. As usual, there is too much tension and raw nerves are stretched almost to the breaking point. Everyone knows that some will not survive the next few weeks.

8
The Death of General Rose

THE BREAKOUT FROM THE BRIDGEHEAD on the Rhine in March 1945 was similar in many ways to the breakout at St. Lô the previous July. As before, there was an initial overwhelming thrust at a specific point on the front, in this case the Remagen bridgehead. This was followed by a very rapid push by the U.S. First Army's VII Corps (led, in part, by the 3rd Armored Division) east as far as Marburg, then north to Paderborn and Lippstadt to link up with the 2nd Armored Division of the U.S. Ninth Army, which had been pushing slowly eastward from the area of Wesel. This linkup cut off and ultimately forced the surrender of 325,000 German troops of Army Group B, who had been trapped in the Ruhr district by the rapid American advance. In this way it duplicated the closing of the Argentan–Falaise gap after the St. Lô breakout, though it was much more successful this time because German resistance was a shadow of what it had been seven months before.

Willis's diary entries for this period parallel those of the rapid American drive across France, and they offer two illustrations of the dangers such operations entailed for the individuals involved. In the first, Major General Maurice Rose, the commander of the 3rd Armored Division, was in a detachment of two jeeps, two motorcycles, and an armored car that was moving between two of the division's task forces on the evening of March 30. The column was attacked by a German tank and infantry force that had been bypassed in the drive toward the city. General Rose's party was captured by a German tank crew, and the general was apparently shot by one of the nervous crewmen. In the second incident, Willis himself was involved in an ambush by another force of bypassed German tanks and infantry while he was part of a resupply convoy on the 150-mile trip back to the supply dumps in the Rhine bridgehead. The two incidents are reminders that surrounded or bypassed German units did not generally just surrender but pursued a counterattack designed to break out of the encirclement.

Sunday, March 25, 1945   In the very early morning
hours, the combat commands of the 3rd Armored Division
move out of bivouac. Spearhead columns, with tanks in
front spitting blue flame from their exhausts, lead the way.
Then tank destroyers, followed by infantry, combat engineers, reconnaissance, mobile artillery, signal company,
medics, maintenance, supply, and division trains — all
that make up our division — are on the move. Hundreds of
motors break the stillness of the morning this March day.
The tempo increases until the sound becomes a mighty
roar.

A bright moon is visible on the horizon as the attack
gets under way. The tired and weary faces of the men in the
1st and 104th Infantry gaze up at us as we pass through
their positions. We are now alone, out ahead of all the other
divisions. It is not a good place to be. There is no shouting
among us, only whispers in the dark. A stillness from all,
as if everyone is holding his breath.

No words can describe one's feelings as we move
forward in the darkness on strange roads through enemy
territory. Each has his own individual thoughts. Foremost
is to survive if we can. So many are not with us anymore.
One gets to thinking, how many more chances will I get to
carry me through? We all know what lies ahead. Death and
destruction will soon be among us on our drive. What we
don't know is when, where, and how it will happen.

We encounter scattered resistance in our path. Several tanks and self-propelled guns are destroyed. Our Pershing tank is proving to be a good fighting machine. But, as
usual, soon some of our tanks are burning, and the
wounded are being evacuated by the medics.

As our forces move slowly forward, a German airfield
is seen to the left of our convoy. The field is littered with
hulks of destroyed planes and parts, the results of the
heavy bombings by our air fleets. Some areas are covered
with holes of various sizes.

Monday, March 26, 1945   Luck was with me again

this morning. We received a heavy barrage of mortar shells. One shell landed a few feet from where we were standing. Four of us got into a large hole which was nearby. After the explosion we found no one was injured. Mortars give very little warning before arriving at their destination.

Our division is taking hundreds of prisoners. We are, however, still encountering very heavy resistance in many German towns. With continuing clear skies, the P-47 Thunderbolts have been extremely helpful in destroying enemy armor. Although at times we receive heavy artillery fire, most of the enemy defense seems to be rear guard action.

The weather is warm as spring approaches. It is a sharp contrast to the freezing blizzards of the Ardennes last winter.

Tuesday, March 27, 1945   The 3rd Armored Division broke through enemy defenses today. We are moving fast as town after town falls before our assault. Seems almost impossible that we could be covering this much ground in our advance. This is similar to the breakthrough at St. Lô. Clouds of dust cover our route as we push forward.

As I glance around at my buddies wearing goggles, I am reminded of science fiction, for they look like men from Mars. Cakes of dust and sweat cover us. Many bottles of cognac are emptied on this drive.

Our route is becoming littered with many enemy tanks and other vehicles. The deadly P-47 Thunderbolts have spotted some German convoys and are raining destruction upon them.

As we drive ever deeper into the center of Germany, another spectacle is before us. The slave laborers of Europe are everywhere on the roads, sometimes causing traffic jams in our convoy. They trudge happily to the rear, waving and shouting to us. They seem to be in very poor health and all are walking.

Record numbers of enemy are being captured. So many that at times we don't have the means or time to bother with them. Many seem glad to surrender, but by no means are they all quitting. Still very hard fighting and hardships are ahead for our troops.

Wednesday, March 28, 1945   Our ammunition train made a hurried trip to the rear area for more war supplies. Roads are jammed with troops moving up to the front. It is very dangerous on these trips, as many of the bypassed areas are still held by enemy troops. We have no heavy armor or large guns, so we must depend on speed and machine guns. When attacked, our troops rake the terrain with a heavy field of fire.

Thursday, March 29, 1945   This cloudy, overcast day finds our forces on the roads, driving ever forward. Some of the towns we pass through have not been touched by war, but later in the day we see more black smoke on the horizon. Tanks from our task forces are facing large Tiger tanks and the dreaded 128 mm guns, so once more we are confronted by a stubborn and suicidal enemy.

I'm getting tired and sleepy, as we have had no rest the past few days. Sure do hope we get a break soon.

As night descends, we learn our journey has been a long one this March day. The 3rd Armored Division has advanced over one hundred miles against the enemy in a single day. The greatest one-day advance in the history of mobile warfare.

Friday, March 30, 1945   After the record drive by our division yesterday, we now encounter very stubborn opposition. As our spearhead columns approach Kirchborchen, we learn the place is full of Death's Head SS troops. Immediately our tankers encounter a heavy concentration of fire from bazooka teams. As always when faced by fanatical Nazi soldiers, the result is a very savage battle. The streets are scenes of smoke and flames as we move slowly forward. Many of our Sherman tanks are burning from the accurate fire of the German 88s.

From attics, cellars, and ruins the black-garbed SS suicide teams use all of their tactics to halt our advance. No quarter is given and none is asked in this deadly game of life and death. Here we are pitted against the best of Hitler's troops. Everywhere we hear the angry whine of machine-gun bullets and small-arms fire.

In the face of this man-made hell, the infantry once more moves ahead to secure the ground. And as has happened so many times before, again many are dying as the battle rages in this small town.

Our artillery fire is thunderous as it is called upon to help overcome enemy strongholds. Loud explosions followed by smoke and fire mark the site of targets hit by our long-range guns. As the buildings crumble in our path, we drive into the burning town.

Today we are fortunate to have the help of our Thunderbolts. Their presence in the clear skies saves many lives. To me they seem like the swallows that we have back home, diving and soaring around the chimneys. However, here is a much deadlier attack and far more dangerous. In perfect formation the P-47s peel off into screaming dives in the face of heavy enemy fire. Loud explosions echo through the town, and black smoke can be seen rising from burning Tiger tanks.

This action is not without cost to our friends in the sky. Even now as I watch this air spectacle, one of our planes is hit and explodes with a roar. The charred and burning plane falls to earth in many pieces. This event seems very much like the fireworks back home on the Fourth of July, but it is not the same. There is no one in the rockets back home when they explode.

Later, in the evening, we receive the tragic news that General Rose has been killed. This occurred as he was riding in his peep up to the front line. An enemy force of Tiger tanks had closed the road behind one of our task forces. General Rose and two of his staff drove into an ambush. Few details are available at this time as to what really happened. We saw heavy machine-gun fire earlier on this road.

As night descends, we have orders to leave for another load of gas and ammunition. The round-trip is now three hundred miles. There will be no sleep for us tonight. At midnight we move out on the long journey for supplies. Progress is slow, as only blackout lights can be used for driving. Soon the sound of battle fades away and we are alone on the road. Only the sound of motors can be heard on this quiet night. The beginning of our trip is kind of spooky as I peer into the darkness from behind my machine-gun turret. Some trains never return from their trips after supplies. Isolated pockets of enemy troops are all along our route to the rear. Our convoy is not very large — only thirty vehicles and nearly sixty troops. Our only protection is our machine guns and basic weapons.

Saturday, March 31, 1945   After traveling all day, our convoy finally stops in a small German town. The foul weather is bringing a cold rain. After searching for a time, we find shelter in some homes. Our crew is lucky in getting sleeping quarters in a home whose owner is an American. In talking with him, we learn his wife is German. They had been on a visit to her homeland when the war came. Although they have been treated well, the authorities would not allow them to leave the country. Our host has an inexhaustible supply of white wine, which makes the evening pass very quickly. Finally, after posting guards we unroll our bedrolls and try getting some rest. Soon all is quiet in the house. In a few minutes, due to the quietness, I sleep soundly.

Sometime later I waken with a start to realize I had been dreaming. The dream seemed so real. Driving along the road, our convoy comes to the foot of a large mountain. After traveling for a time, we near the crest of the incline. Suddenly German tanks and infantry appear and commence firing at us. Amid the confusion and excitement, I awake. Quickly sitting up, I look around the large room. All of my comrades are sleeping and the house is quiet. Sheepishly, I lay back into my blankets. But in spite of my attempts to sleep, I get very little rest. Each time I doze off, the same dream returns to bother me.

Sunday, April 1, 1945   When daylight comes, I've had very little sleep. As we prepare to leave on our journey, I very quickly relate my strange dream to my crew. Bowden has a good laugh while informing me that I'd been watching too many war movies.

After a quick meal of K rations, our convoy moves out on the roads. It is a beautiful Easter morning. Would be very easy to forget our mission amid these quiet surroundings. As we continue on our trip, a strange feeling creeps over me. I try to reason with myself — no doubt my dream has upset me.

We all sense something is wrong. There is no sign of life as our forces move through the towns. Soon we reach a crossroad. We turn to the right and continue on our way. After turning a sharp corner, we are brought to a sudden stop. Ahead are two large trees lying across the road in our path. A short delay and the road is cleared; again we move forward.

Everyone in our column is now beginning to feel uneasy. We have seen no friendly troops for several hours. Upon reaching the top of a small hill, we see a small village ahead of us. Large clouds of dust rise from among the buildings. Sgt. Laszchuck passes us moving to the front of our column. I see him standing and waving his arms. Reaching the first vehicle, he stops in the center of the road. Quickly he climbs into the lead peep while passing his field glasses to Sgt. Rivard. After a long look toward the village, Sgt. Rivard makes a gesture for all to turn around. We are informed that the town directly ahead is filled with German troops. It doesn't take long to get the message and less time to carry out the orders. Within a few minutes, we are traveling back down the road we just came over. This time we are moving at a much faster pace.

After covering several miles, a halt is called. Several of the sergeants hold a conference to decide which route to take. No one will admit openly that we are lost. We are ordered to return to the last crossroad. Arriving there, we then turn to the left and continue several miles before seeing any sign of life.

A short time later our column finds a group of Sherman tanks on the road. We are glad to see them but their company is brief, as soon they turn off and we are alone again. A few hours later we are joined by a small unit which consists of a peep and two armored cars. Their captain assumes command of the convoy.

Our progress is much slower, as a rugged mountain range is now in front of our route. Much of the terrain is thick brush, which must be scouted before we can proceed. A small village lies ahead of our convoy. Entering the quiet, narrow streets, we discover that there are no people visible among the buildings. I crouch behind my machine gun trying to detect signs of life or movement from this enemy town. As we near the edge of this place, we are surprised to find an infantry regiment of the 108th Division digging in to form a fortification. Even more amazing is that this force is facing the direction we are traveling. Upon questioning their captain, we learn they are getting prepared for trouble but have seen no Germans.

After another hurried conference, a decision is made for all to continue on our route. By now our convoy is nearly a mile long. As we begin driving up the steep mountain, Glover tells his crew that this would be a bad place to meet Tiger tanks. His remark does not seem very funny to me.

As the front of our convoy nears the crest of the mountain, a shot rings out over the quiet countryside. This is followed by several bursts of rapid machine-gun fire. Each of us has his own version of what is taking place ahead of us. Bowden tells me someone is getting trigger-happy. But as I glance around the mountainside, I get a sinking sensation in my stomach. Then it hits me like a thunderbolt — my dream. The mountains and everything look the same as they had last night. I keep thinking this can't be. After all, it was only a bad nightmare. My hopes are shattered a few minutes later as one of our motorcycle scouts passes us on his way to the rear of the convoy. He is but a blur on the road, so swift is this messenger of ill news. But we all hear his fateful message clearly this

Easter Sunday. His voice rings out over the quiet mountain: "Tanks! Tanks! Everywhere are German troops! Turn
around!" We learn later his heroic action saved many of our
lives. Within a very few minutes our orderly convoy is
turned into a mass of confusion and destruction. The
narrow mountain road is almost impossible for us to turn
around on; several trucks upset in the attempt.

The enemy had cunningly waited until we were all
climbing the narrow mountain road before attacking.
Having destroyed both armored cars and the lead peep in
their surprise assault, now they are closing in for the kill.

Glover, not being able to turn around, decides on
another route. Turning the steering wheel sharply, he
drives our track up a steep bank and into a small field.
Ahead of us is a barbed-wire fence, which snaps like a
ribbon when our heavy war machine is driven through.
After getting back on the road, we continue but a short
distance when we are stopped again. The Germans have
planned their attack very wisely. Having zeroed in their
guns on two sharp curves, they wait until the precise
moment. As soon as the lead gas truck reaches the corner,
it is hit by enemy tank fire. Now our route of escape is a
blazing inferno. Seconds later a second truck explodes
with a roar after it too is disabled. It is now impossible to
continue down the mountain road, and our convoy grinds
to a halt once more.

Everywhere I look the German soldiers are advancing
with their huge tanks. More trucks and tracks are now
burning fiercely as dense clouds of black smoke drift over
us. Glover, realizing we can proceed no farther, drives our
track into the side of a high bank. It doesn't take us long to
understand that our ride is over.

Sgt. Rivard yells for us to form a line of defense. At this
time I grab a bazooka from the rack and hit the ground.
Some of our troops are already firing machine guns at the
oncoming Germans and their tanks. Quickly glancing
around, I count only about a dozen here with me behind
this high bank. It seems hours since the first shot rang

out. Actually, all of this has taken only a few minutes.

Waiting here in the hot sun on this Sunday afternoon, many thoughts race through my head. Is this the end? Our orders are to hold our positions. It seems suicide to try holding off the enemy tanks, as we have no heavy guns. I keep trying to convince myself that this is only a nightmare, but the roar of advancing enemy tanks accompanied by heavy fire soon brings my senses back to reality. As one tank pauses to fire, another one moves ever closer to our small force. It is fast becoming very apparent that there is no way we can stop this large force of German armor. For us to remain here means total annihilation. Soon our sergeant begins to realize that nothing can be gained by remaining. As he crawls along our line, his message is brief: "Every man for himself. Get out the best way you can." We need no urging. Already the large shells are hitting our barricade. Angry machine-gun bullets whiz overhead.

Telling Bowden to follow me, I join several of my buddies moving down the steep mountain slope. The enemy is directing his fire to the front of our small force. Fortunately for us, his fire is not very accurate. After moving through heavy terrain for what seems like hours, we stop for a short rest. At our feet is a small mountain stream. Water never tasted so refreshing to me. We find that our little group numbers seven. Glover is with us, but Bowden is absent. I can only hope he has escaped with another group. We continue over these rugged mountains, hoping to reach friendly troops before night. Very warily we circle several villages in which there is no sign of life. Observing a bright glare shining through the pine trees, we advance cautiously. Soon some of our American troops are visible. After a period of time we finally convince them we are friendly, and they allow us to pass through their lines. After being taken to their headquarters, we relate our version of the ambush to the commanding officer.

In recalling my dream, I can only ponder what significance it had for the events which took place. Why did the events in my dream become a reality the next day? If I was being forewarned, I was powerless to do anything about it. Had I been in command, would I have done differently? I will never know the answer to my questions.

Monday, April 2, 1945   Our small group is still with a regiment of the 108th Infantry Division and a battalion of tank destroyers. Some of their troops are moving forward for the attack against the enemy. Once again we hear the chatter of machine-gun fire in the mountains. Also the explosions of heavy guns echo through the valley, followed by clouds of black smoke rising from the heavy forests.

Happily, we receive the news that more of our troops made their way through enemy lines to safety today. This group had been forced to spend the night in the mountains surrounded by Germans. Nearly half of the troops from our convoy have now been accounted for. All vehicles except one were lost in the ambush. This crew escaped by driving over a high cliff and crossing a small stream.

My friend Bowden is not in the group that arrived today. He had injured his hand while jumping from our track. I'm hoping he was able to escape and will show up later.

Tuesday, April 3, 1945   We are still with the 108th Infantry. We have no means of transportation to join our division. The only equipment with us is our guns and gas masks. The troops are sharing their rations, so no one goes hungry. Each of us is given a blanket, which helps to keep us warm at night. The weather is very cold in the mountains.

Wednesday, April 4, 1945   We have been told that all of our group may be able to leave in a few days. We are anxious to rejoin our own unit.

This area is very rugged country with high mountains and thick forests. Some elements of the 108th Infantry are still fighting the Germans in the heavy terrain nearby.

Thursday, April 5, 1945   After a hurried breakfast with our kind infantry friends, we are ordered to be prepared to move.

Later, loading into trucks, our convoy moves out onto the road. After traveling most of the day, we are happy to see the familiar patch of the 3rd Armored Division.

We are spending the night at Division Rear, where we are issued new gear and equipment from the supply battalion. As night arrives, we receive orders to join our units tomorrow.

Friday, April 6, 1945   After a short journey, we reach our division. There had been some very savage fighting while we were gone. A large number of the Germans were trapped when our division met the 2nd Armored. This pocket is going to be called the Rose Pocket in memory of our general who was killed. Thousands of the enemy were forced to surrender.

Our crew receives a new track and machine guns, as all was lost in the ambush. I am still with Glover on the .50-calibre gun. We have a replacement, since Bowden is not with us. I'm still hoping he got out safely.

As we rejoin our division, a new drive is near for us. Our next objective is the Weser River. Just one more river to cross — have been hearing this ever since we unloaded on the beaches of Normandy.

Saturday, April 7, 1945   Early morning skies are still dark as our spearhead columns move out onto the roads. Reaching the Weser River, we find all of the bridges destroyed. Our engineers build pontoon bridges, then all units cross to the east side. We are receiving scattered artillery fire from the enemy. Our task force columns fan out for the coming attack.

Sunday, April 8, 1945   As the hours roll by, our spearhead drive begins to gain speed. Many towns are taken by our attacking task forces. One tank unit finds and destroys six railroad guns.

The roads are crowded with refugees. Nearly all are walking; some even pull carts with their belongings piled high. Every nationality is seen in this vast group of people. This is a very tragic sight to behold. Our troops pass out food to the children as we move forward. Many of the people are in a very weakened condition. Being here is the only way one can truly understand this terrible happening. These people wander like sheep in a blizzard, with no place to go. Indeed, they have been in a storm and are still caught up in this savage conflict. It is difficult to describe the destruction and devastation that the winds of war have brought to the countries of Europe. The suffering and hardships of these people are almost unbelievable.

This evening, while waiting in convoy, one of our crew observed an old man lying in a ditch. Leaving our track, we walked over to him and found he was in very poor health. Sores matted with lice covered his body, while he was near death from hunger. As our medics treated his sores, several of us fixed him some food, which we left beside him with a canteen of water. He was still waving to us as we turned the next corner.

Monday, April 9, 1945   The stars are still shining in the sky as we are ordered out of our bedrolls. Soon our convoy is back on the road after another supply of ammunition for the firing batteries. Our journey is much quieter this time, as no enemy troops are found. Only a long, hard, grueling ride for all of us.

After loading our tracks, our force is soon back on the road for the return trip. Back at the front, we learn the round-trip has been nearly four hundred miles. I'm one tired soldier, as we have had no sleep.

Tuesday, April 10, 1945   Another bright sunny day finds our columns again driving into the heart of the fatherland of Germany. One of our task forces encounters several enemy antitank guns, which are destroyed. Then reconnaissance patrols find and clear a V-2 rocket assembly plant at Kleinbodungen, where we discover huge rockets being built by the Nazis. After taking more prisoners, an underground shaft is discovered in the assembly plant. This proves to be one of the secret factories. Many tunnels are found below the surface.

The town of Epschenrode is becoming very difficult to capture. Fierce battles are raging in the streets. German troops led by SS officers are putting up stubborn resistance in the path of our troops. The enemy is using bazooka fire, and some of our tanks are burning.

The clear sky is filled with friendly P-47 Thunderbolts. After a period of time during which these planes bomb and strafe enemy strongholds, the buildings crumble into rubble. The remaining enemy forces come out to surrender.

Our spearhead columns are moving out of the town even as the last resistance ceases. As night descends upon us, our spearheads pause on the edge of the city of Nordhausen. Orders have been received to launch an attack at dawn.

This night, while we are bivouacked at the edge of the city, the roar of many planes fills the sky. Soon waves of heavy bombers rain death and destruction upon Nordhausen.

9

Death Camp

ON APRIL 11, 1945, the troops of the 3rd Armored Division discovered a tragedy worse than any of the carnage from the fighting they had witnessed since D-Day: the death camp at Nordhausen. Formally named Boelke Kaserne, Nordhausen was a subcamp of the nearby and larger camp at Dora, which was a labor camp for the assembly of V-1 and V-2 rockets in deep underground tunnels. While Nordhausen supplied some of the labor for the work at Dora, on the whole the prisoners at the subcamp were apparently expected simply to die. Conditions at Nordhausen and Dora were considered among the worst at any of the Nazi death camps. Clearly, the conditions the Allied troops found there left them with memories they would not forget as the war swept eastward.

Willis continued to serve in the division's ammunition train, though by now the danger from bypassed German troops had been recognized and the convoys were more heavily escorted. As a result, most of the fighting Willis describes is from the viewpoint of an observer at some distance, no doubt to his relief. One of the events he observed firsthand, however, was the steady stream of civilian refugees pouring westward away from the fighting — and also away from the advancing Russian armies farther east. Both the German refugees and the German troops who were now surrendering by the thousands sought safety behind the Allied lines. Then, too, Willis himself, realizing that the war in Europe was winding down, began to express in his diary an interest in not gaining the dubious honor of being the last soldier to die in combat in the European theater.

Wednesday, April 11, 1945   As dawn is breaking in the east, our forces push forward into Nordhausen. We are encountering very little resistance in our probing attacks, but we do find something that none of us expected.

Nordhausen! Death Camp! Hell Hole! It is very difficult

to describe what we find. Of all the terrible war action we have witnessed in the past year, none can compare with this tragedy. Nordhausen — a slave extermination camp — is just that! People are lying everywhere by the hundreds. Living and dead are together in many cases. We are finding it very difficult to distinguish one from the other. Only by the flicker of an eyelid or the twitch of the body can one tell. Many are in barracks, which cover the compound. Some are naked, piled high like so much cordwood in the corners and under stairways. Others are found outside, throughout the many acres of this vast camp. Over all of this slave extermination place can be heard the moan and whimper of the dying. Very few can walk, but some totter about as in a dreamworld. The stench of decomposing bodies is almost unbelievable in this carnal place. Only by sheer willpower can we continue our grim task of separating the dead from the living. Many lie where they were mowed down with machine guns by SS guards. This was their fate as they tried to find shelter from last night's air raid.

We find slaves from nearly every country of Europe. The authorities of Nordhausen and Dora, a city which is north of here, had a very efficient program. The slaves, surrounded by high barbed-wire fences and guarded by ruthless SS troops, worked on V-1 and V-2 assembly lines. Black bread and thin soup were their once-a-day meal, which was near the starvation level.

The sadistic guards had a sure and final cure for slackers and the sick. Every morning they hung thirty-two slaves and forced the entire camp to watch. In Dora the cremation ovens were always hot and ready.

Never before have I seen the look that is in the eyes of these people. They are so thankful as they gaze at us. We are doing all that we can to care for them, but for many our help is too late.

Thursday, April 12, 1945   Another chapter is unfolding, which we are again to witness. Our engineers, using bulldozers, are digging deep holes in the earth. Upon receiving orders from our officers, the German civilians are ordered to bury the dead slaves. This is proving to be a very grim task. This horrible spectacle is another reminder of the cruel and inhuman treatment of the people of Europe by the evil Nazi regime.

At evening we leave this city of death. All are upset by what we have seen the past two days. The mood of the troops is tempered as our spearhead columns drive forward toward new battles.

Glancing around the quiet countryside, we are moving out of the Harz Mountains. Our forces reach the Saale River and find these bridges all destroyed. Although we are temporarily delayed, the engineers soon construct bridges and we cross to the east side of the stream.

Friday, April 13, 1945   At dawn, our division leaves the Harz Mountains and races forward into the open plains. Eisleben lies ahead of our forces. It has been declared an open city.

Soon we enter Polleben, a German prisoner-of-war camp. We liberate several hundred Englishmen. It has been a long wait for many, having been captured several years ago. Cheers fill the air as our battle groups thunder down the narrow cobblestone streets. Many Englishmen are so happy they break down and cry. It is a very emotional scene to behold.

Driving into the next town, a raging fire is burning out of control. Our crew is lucky to find a shelter in a building that is still standing. Part of the troops are forced to move out of town in order to find a place to bivouac.

Saturday, April 14, 1945   Morning finds our track back on the road after another load of ammunition. I'm still machine gunner in the turret on the .50-calibre gun. Spillman, who is now the third member of our crew, was also with me on the second antitank gun. There are now many replacements in our division.

While on this trip, we managed to become lost again.

After driving through three towns where there was no sign of life, we decided to turn around. Returning to the last crossroad, we took the other route, which proved to be correct. We arrived at our destination safely.

Returning to the front, we find our spearheads have driven forward from the bridgehead on the Saale River.

We find every town being turned into a fortress by fanatic enemy groups, who many times defend to the death. Still more furious and deadly battles loom ahead for us on our drive.

Sunday, April 15, 1945   Our crew had no sleep last night, as we made a quick trip to one of the batteries. C Battery was low on ammunition and we were ordered to supply them.

Some of their large guns were firing directly on last-ditch defenders. While on this trip, bullets ricocheted against our track, which added to the hectic mission. Again resistance is increasing all along the front.

Monday, April 16, 1945   Another day finds me with our train going back for more ammunition. Our convoy is very large, consisting of armored cars and light tanks. The extra firepower is very welcome to us. Still many enemy pockets are in the rear areas, as our infantry divisions have not been able to keep up with our armor.

The rubber on our tracks is wearing out due to the high mileage and heavy use of the past year. When the tracks fall apart, we have no time to repair them. These vehicles are abandoned and the crew climbs into another track. To remain on the road would be suicide, as Germans are everywhere in the forests and towns.

Tuesday, April 17, 1945   Our convoy had several firefights on our return. After having received sniper fire in several towns we passed through, we received orders to return the fire. The next few hours found our forces moving through the streets with all of our guns blazing. Although the exchange was heavy, no one was injured.

A large number of enemy troops attacked and overran a command post at Thurland while we were gone. It was a slaughter, as they turned their large Panzerfaust bazookas on each house where our troops were billeted last night.

Thurland is a peaceful-looking village in the morning sunlight, surrounded by the green countryside. Appearances are deceiving as our reconnaissance battalions, supported by tanks and other units, move forward in attack. Soon they encounter a withering fire from the fortified positions of the enemy. Now the full force of concentrated fire from our artillery batteries is brought to bear on the German defenses. Billowing clouds of dust and smoke are visible rolling up into the blue sky. Raging fires cover the village. However, bitter fighting continues in this small town. The enemy captured some of our tanks and armored cars in last night's battle. This adds to the confusion. Many of these troops are fanatics and will not surrender. In coping with this situation, many of our troops are dying as the savage battle intensifies during this long day.

At evening we leave the burning village behind. The Mulde River is before our spearheaders. After several attempts by our engineers to build bridges across the stream, orders cancel the operation. Very heavy mortar and artillery fire is being directed on us.

We see thousands of slave laborers, displaced persons, and Allied prisoners in our midst. All are cluttering the roads and in many cases raiding stores and homes. This problem is becoming very difficult for us. Our immediate concern is ending the war, and so far this has not happened.

As the war seems to be nearing an end, all seem to have the same thought: If I can just hang on for a few more days. There is a new look in everyone's eyes, as we hope the war will be over real soon.

Wednesday, April 18, 1945   This morning we are moving ahead very slowly. The villages are being defended by obstinate Germans. What we had hoped would be light opposition toward the end of hostilities is proving to be otherwise.

Entering the village of Bobbau-Steinfurth, nicknamed "Bobby Sox" by one task force, it soon becomes a scene of fierce fighting. After repeated attempts to take the village, artillery fire is called for to help break the enemy fortifications. The heavy shelling by our firing batteries cannot dislodge the enemy. Twelve P-47s are in the clear sky above our positions. As we watch our friends in the sky, their dangerous mission of diving into the face of heavy antiaircraft fire begins. The rain of bombs sends sheets of flame and black smoke into the air. Several enemy tanks are hit, and fire can be seen rising from their iron hulks.

Adding to this already-burning village, an enemy gas dump is set on fire. Flames are shooting hundreds of feet into the clear sky as the area becomes an inferno. The heat of the roaring flames can be felt from where we stand.

Thursday, April 19, 1945   This morning I decided to start digging in the ground for shelter in case I have need of it. I'm either becoming careless or lazy, as I've not picked up a shovel for a long time.

Those German 88s are getting too close for comfort. Since the war is winding down, I'm not taking any unnecessary chances these last few days. I've noticed some of my buddies have the same idea.

Friday, April 20, 1945   Some good news for all the troops. Our mail has finally caught up to us. This is always a sure sign our sector is becoming safer. Received several letters, including one from Mom. Was very glad to hear from home.

Everyone is saying that the war is nearly over. I don't know. It is almost too much for me to believe. Anyway, this is the main topic of conversation here. No one wants to take any unnecessary risks now.

10

The Final Battle

WITH SO LITTLE OF GERMANY LEFT between the Allied and Russian forces, and with advances through this sector so rapid, Willis and the other troops of the 3rd Armored Division could be fairly confident that the assault on Dessau would be the last battle they would face. They were at the end of the long road that stretched back to Normandy. So many thousands of German troops were anxious to surrender that the occupation of this one last city might have been expected to be a fairly simple operation. But, as had so often been the case since the division had broken out of the Remagen bridgehead in March, mixed with the majority of German troops who had no more stomach for fighting was a fanatical group determined to continue the war to the bitter end. In this case the determined resistance came from the officer candidates and noncommissioned officers of the Rosslau-Dessau combat engineering school, who offered the 3rd Armored Division one final lesson in the skillful preparation of layered defenses and accurate marksmanship. American troop strength and ordnance were simply overwhelming by this stage, however, and the outcome was never really in doubt.

With the surrender of the last remaining German troops in Dessau, Willis's division was relieved by the 9th Infantry Division. The 3rd Armored Division went first into reserve and then — after the formal surrender of the German forces took effect on May 8 — into the welcome status of occupation troops in a Germany at peace.

Saturday, April 21, 1945   Soon after dawn we have orders to begin the assault on the city of Dessau. All of the troops are very nervous, as we well know this could be our last battle. Already Russian shells are falling beyond the Elbe River. These last days of the war are no more pleasant than the first ones back in Normandy, which seems ages ago.

Our heavy field artillery batteries are in position. At a given signal a thunderous barrage opens up the attack. Hundreds of guns are heard as our attack begins. Flames and smoke are rising from within the city. Armored tanks and infantry push slowly forward to the edge of this large town. Their attack is halted by the dreaded bazooka. The savage fighting is developing into a bloody house-to-house battle. The infantry forces are obliged to resort to search-and-destroy tactics in clearing the city of enemy troops.

Although the end of hostilities seems near, this battle is one of our bloodiest. The cost of life is very high as our task forces move through the ruins.

Everyone was hoping the victory here would be easy and many lives could be saved, but this wasn't to be. Many of our buddies die in the closing days of the war in this conclusive battle.

Sunday, April 22, 1945   Sunrise shows more doughs and tanks being used, as resistance is increasing. We are very busy today trying to keep ammunition supplied to our field artillery guns.

As darkness descends, sharp and bitter battles still rage throughout the city. The dark night is made as light as day by massive gunfire. Added to this is the chatter of machine guns as red tracers stream across the sky. It seems to me as if the long night will never end in this our last battle.

Monday, April 23, 1945   Dessau falls to our forces today. This ultimate battle near the end of the war was one of the bloodiest for the 3rd Armored Division. Many snipers are being rounded up throughout the ruins. We found two of our engineers dead nearby this morning. Each had a bullet in his head. We must be on guard constantly and avoid being alone.

Tuesday, April 24, 1945   Dessau is very quiet now. The streets are covered with rubble from shattered homes and other buildings. Smoke is still rising from charred hulks of tanks. Some civilians are on the streets as the massive cleanup begins.

Rumors are heard among the troops. Meeting the Russians is the main topic of conversation. No one knows for sure what our next move will be as we await new orders. Everyone is tired, including me. I will sleep for a week if I ever get the chance.

Wednesday, April 25, 1945   Good news! The 3rd Armored Division is being relieved by the 9th Infantry. Our orders are to pull back from the front line. Soon we are on the road in a long convoy. By evening we have covered fifty miles.

A combat soldier has three things to look forward to: wounds, death, or the end of hostilities. To all of us, the last seemed to be only a dream during the past year.

Thursday, April 26, 1945   We camped in a meadow last night. Just sat around and talked, something we have not had time to do for a long time.

I'm spending the day cleaning and trying to rest. I am so keyed up it may take years to completely relax, but all have the same problem. I wanted to sleep the clock around last night, but must have wakened a hundred times.

Friday, April 27, 1945   Took in a movie last night with Irish and Glover. Our battery has a projector set up in an old building. It was a good picture. The first we had seen for a long time.

This place is very different from those of just a few days ago. It is so quiet I find myself listening, and there is nothing to hear. It is nice, though, as if we have suddenly been transferred to another world.

The morning sun is shining brightly on the green meadows. Birds are seen flying through the trees as they sing. Some rabbits and other small animals are playing in the grass. To many people, these small events might not seem very important, but to us who have survived the war, this means a great part of our lives is now being returned to us. It has been so long since we have been able to observe the little things in life that really are the main concern of all. It is everyone's hope that we can once more take up our lives and begin to live in peace.

Saturday, April 28, 1945   We are billeted in a small, peaceful village. Sure is nice after some of our past living quarters. Our crew is in a nice brick home. Don't know how long we will be here, but it is extra nice now.

The Germans we meet are not very friendly, which is fine with me. We have not been on a friendship tour of Germany.

Sunday, April 29, 1945   Another day finds me taking things easy, as is nearly everyone else. Received many letters today. Some were over two months old. Ended up the evening by answering as many as I had time to write.

I'm trying to keep away from guard duty and detail work. I have been lucky so far, as I've had plenty of experience.

Monday, April 30, 1945   Our division has orders to move. A few hours later finds our convoy back on the dry, dusty roads. Our next destination is sixty miles to the south of here. We move through some very nice country-side. No ravages of war are seen in this part of Germany. Much of it is as I remember the rural areas of Iowa.

Near evening we finally reach Sangerhausen, south of the Harz Mountains. We are staying in nice homes again.

Tuesday, May 1, 1945   At last they have caught up with me. I'm back on KP at the kitchen. It has taken a long time. This is the second time since leaving England nearly a year ago. I really don't mind, as the food is good — much tastier than we used to cook while on the antitank gun. The duty here gives me time to visit with some of my buddies, who are cooks.

Not much going on, as we are waiting for the war to end.

Wednesday, May 2, 1945   Irish and I took some pictures with his camera. Will be several months before they are returned to us from processing. Makes no difference, as we have plenty of time and don't seem to be going anywhere soon.

The brass is becoming much stricter again. Orders are to start shaving every day. I am not in favor of this rule but have no choice.

Thursday, May 3, 1945   All equipment is being washed and cleaned. We are to have a big inspection this Saturday. Seems to be a lot of griping about this news. We have not had this duty since England. There wasn't any time until now.

Friday, May 4, 1945   Took in another movie along with some of my friends. It is good recreation, very different from what we have been having.

This town is full of pretty frauleins — a smile to one's face and a knife in the back. I'm not planning on becoming too friendly.

Saturday, May 5, 1945   The news sounds good, as the Germans are surrendering everywhere. We hope the war will be over soon. No one wants to see any more action — we have had our share.

Sunday, May 6, 1945   Irish and I are on a tour of the town. Sure looks peaceful, but we still have our guns in case we need them. Everyone has learned to trust only our troops over here. Many Americans were slain by civilians during the long journey from the beaches of Normandy.

Monday, May 7, 1945   Rumors are that the war is nearly over. At least it sounds good, and I sure hope it is true.

No one is doing very much, as we are just waiting for the good news. Except when on guard duty, we do about as we please.

Tuesday, May 8, 1945   THE WAR IS OVER! Thank God for that! I only hope it was not in vain, as the price was very high.

Many of our buddies are not here at the end as we lay down our weapons. As I look around, many new faces are visible. A large number of the familiar ones are absent. It is a hollow victory for many families.

Wednesday, May 9, 1945   No one is celebrating the end of the war. We are glad, yes! But as we look back over the past year there are too many bitter memories for us to have a good time now. Maybe, someday, all will feel different, but now it is too soon.

And where do we go from here? The war against Japan is still going on. No one knows what will happen to our division. Everyone is hoping for the best.

Thursday, May 10, 1945   Today we found that our division is located in territory that the Russians are to occupy. We will be moving soon.

The only duty we have now is pulling guard. I may be able to gain some weight if this easy life-style continues. The hard life has left most of the troops lean and mean. I hope that this will change for the better.

Friday, May 11, 1945   Our division received orders to move. All units are on the dusty highway moving south. The country is very pretty, with large forests and many streams.

At last our convoy stops for the night and we camp in a meadow. Seems strange not having a blackout, as we have been in the dark for such a long time. Some of the troops are building large fires. The mood of all seems to be relaxing some.

Saturday, May 12, 1945   Late this day we reach Frankfurt, which is also in ruins. The massive air raids by our heavy bombing fleets have reduced much of the city to rubble. Large machines are starting the massive cleanup job.

Finally we reach a small village as night falls. We are told this is to be our new home.

Sunday, May 13, 1945   All of our battalion is billeted in fine brick homes. The civilians are gone from this area. Nothing is disturbed in this small town, which looks much like some back in the States. In the front yard of each home is a large flagpole, but the flag is missing.

Monday, May 14, 1945   I'm spending much of my time in answering my mail. I have quite a few letters to write now that I have extra time.

Also busy trying to get all of my clothes washed. It is quite a chore, as some have been dirty for months. We hope that a laundry can be found, as no one is very keen on this chore.

Tuesday, May 15, 1945   This area is very nice. Have taken a few trips around the town. We are surrounded on all sides by heavy forests. Most of the trees are in rows as if they had been planted. There are numerous trails throughout the heavy woods. Many of the streams have lots of fish and turtles in them.

Wednesday, May 16, 1945   We are busy cleaning and repairing all the vehicles and guns. Sure hope we never have to use them again. Looks as if an inspection may be in the near future.

When are we going home? No one even wants to talk about Japan. Maybe we will not have to go there after all.

Thursday, May 17, 1945   Every day finds things getting better. Our battery is getting a beer hall close by our area. Also, we have a different movie each night, just like back home — well, not quite.

All of this is a very sudden change from what we have been used to this past year.

Friday, May 18, 1945   There are so many rumors around that no one knows what to believe. I am not going to listen to any of them. One of the more popular ones is that our division will be the occupation troops in Germany. I sure hope that one is false, but I don't want to go to Japan either. The only country I want to see is the United States.

Saturday, May 19, 1945   Went swimming along with some of my buddies today. The pool we used was very modern. It had been the property of the SS troops for years. The water was cold, but I didn't mind. We wanted to relax and have a good time again.

After our swim, we had to walk several miles back to the village where we are living. I even enjoyed that part of our trip.

Sunday, May 20, 1945   I'm just taking things slow and easy and trying to relax. We have no duty except guard and KP. Most of the evening is passed by playing poker or reading.

Most of this small town where we are billeted is off-limits to all troops. Convoys are going into Frankfurt every day. There isn't much we can do when we get there. A lot of heavy equipment is now arriving in the city to begin the cleanup.

Monday, May 21, 1945   I'm back on guard. It isn't too bad, except for the loss of sleep, which I could use. Doubt if I ever get caught up on my rest.

The civilians are becoming friendlier. They all blame Hitler for their misfortune and the war. There isn't a Nazi to be found anywhere in Germany.

Tuesday, May 22, 1945   Things are getting better around here once more. Received several more loads of liquor for the troops. Doesn't taste too good, but we don't have to pay for it. I always heard German beer was the best, but this beverage leaves something to be desired.

Wednesday, May 23, 1945   It is a very warm spring day. The sun is shining as I look forward to one more day of leisure. Looks like a good time for me to go swimming. Spent most of the afternoon at the gravel pit swimming. Sure was crowded. Mostly soldiers and girls on the beach. Not many of our troops can speak German, but they seem to do a good job trying. There were several officers at the beach who had removed their bars.

The troops are still not allowed to fraternize with the enemy. There must not be any enemy around, as that rule doesn't seem to be working.

Thursday, May 24, 1945   Everything is moving very slowly. We have too much time on our hands with nothing to do. Still, there is very little recreation.

In talking to several of my buddies, I've yet to find anyone who plans on remaining in the United States Army. All have reached the same decision on this issue.

Friday, May 25, 1945   The days are dragging by. However, we spend most of our time doing as we please. Time seems to stand still. It is as if we have been in Europe for a lifetime. Everyone is just waiting until we receive orders for our next move.

Saturday, May 26, 1945   Some of my buddies left on pass for Holland today. I would like to visit Switzerland if there are any passes available. Since I was one of the few who were able to visit Paris, I will probably not even ask for leave now.

Sunday, May 27, 1945   Rumors again! Some of our troops may be transferred to another division. Also, that we are in line for more battle stars. I'm hoping to have enough points to go home.

Monday, May 28, 1945   Good news! The 3rd Armored "Spearhead" Division will receive two more battle stars. That will make a total of five campaigns for all of the troops that landed at Omaha Beach. I will not have to go to Japan and will be able to get out of this man's army.

Tuesday, May 29, 1945   Irish and I went into Frankfurt on a night pass for a few hours. Had a fairly good time, considering how things are here. Spent some time at the American Red Cross, which was real nice. From what I see, I'll have no problem adjusting to civilian life.

Wednesday, May 30, 1945   We are hoping to be back in the States before winter. Don't know how these civilians will survive the bad weather without shelter and with very little food. Our troops give the children food from our meals. Some are in very poor physical condition. The war wasn't their fault.

Thursday, May 31, 1945   We are back in school again. The army is holding classes so that we have something to do with our idle time. Seems to help make the day pass quicker. No one is learning very much in the classroom, though. I'm sure now that I must get out of this army.

Friday, June 1, 1945   We have been told that we will be here for Christmas. Sure hope that information is false, as

I'm not looking forward to spending the holidays in Germany.

Irish keeps saying that we will all be home soon. He is certainly thinking positive, which is good.

Saturday, June 2, 1945   A heavy rain greets me as I crawl out of my bedroll. At least we are in out of the damp weather. Spent most of the day reading and sleeping. I may never get caught up on my rest, but I'm sure trying. Did manage to go to the mess hall for my meals, as our catering service isn't very good.

Sunday, June 3, 1945   Morning mail call brings me more letters. I used most of the day to try answering them.

May go fishing one of these days if I can find some gear. Some of the men have gone and have had real good luck.

Monday, June 4, 1945   I'm back on guard duty. Seems to me my turn is coming up real regularly. Someone must think I am a good soldier.

We have some new rules. We may have to start wearing ties again, and I can't find mine. I'm sure the army will furnish me a new one.

Tuesday, June 5, 1945   My long year with the 3rd Armored "Spearhead" Division from D-Day is now over. I am one of the lucky survivors at the end of the war. Many of my friends were not so fortunate.

The nightmare is over for all of us, but we can never forget the horror we went through. Our buddies were young, also, but they fell along the long, hard road from Omaha Beach in Normandy to Dessau, Germany, on the Elbe River. We cursed, shed a few tears, shrugged our shoulders, and went on our way. There was nothing else we could do, but the scar remains with us. I am one year older. To me it seemed like an eternity.

A Note on Sources

The illustrations in this book have been reproduced from Frank Woolner and Murray H. Fowler, *Spearhead in the West, 1941–45: The Third Armored Division* (The Division, 1945); *The XX Corps: Its History and Service in World War II* (The XX Corps Association, 1952); and U.S. War Department, General Staff, St.-Lô *(7 July–19 July 1944)* (Washington, D.C.: Historical Division, War Department, 1947). Among the works consulted in the preparation of the introductions to the book and the individual chapters, the most valuable was *Spearhead in the West*. Also useful were Charles M. Baily, *Faint Praise: American Tanks and Tank Destroyers during World War II* (Hamden, Conn.: Shoestring Press, Archon Books, 1983); Anthony Cave Brown, *Bodyguard of Lies* (New York: Harper and Row, 1975); Konnilyn G. Feig, *Hitler's Death Camps: The Sanity of Madness* (New York: Holmes and Meier, 1979); B. H. Liddell Hart, *History of the Second World War* (New York: G. P. Putnam's Sons, 1970); Max Hastings, *Overlord: D-Day and the Battle for Normandy* (New York: Simon and Schuster, 1984); Ian V. Hogg, *The Guns: 1939–45* (New York: Ballantine Books, 1970); John Keegan, *Six Armies in Normandy: From D-Day to the Liberation of Paris, June 6th–August 25th, 1944* (New York: Viking Press, 1982); Charles B. MacDonald, *The Battle of the Huertgen Forest* (Philadelphia and New York: J. B. Lippincott, 1963); Charles B. MacDonald, *A Time for Trumpets: The Untold Story of the Battle of the Bulge* (New York: William Morrow and Co., 1985).

INDEX